Pastoral Care in Practice

'One of the key markers of a healthy church is that all those connected with it are cared for. While the nature of that care may have changed over the years, this book is a timely reminder of the importance and power of good care, reflecting God's love, through the community of faith. It provides practical advice for those who are new to a caring role, but also timely reminders to those with more experience. Using scripture and experience as a base, it encourages the reader to reflect on and pray about their own calling to the pastoral ministry, whether formal or not.'

The Revd Clare Downing, former Moderator of the General Assembly of the United Reformed Church

'All disciples of Jesus Christ are called to care for one another, whether they have a formal role or not. This is a book in which Michael Hopkins offers a tool for churches, groups and individuals, in any Christian tradition, to develop that care in practical ways which are based upon sound theological foundations and pastoral experience. It is offered in a straightforward format that both supports and challenges the ways in which pastoral care takes place in formal and informal settings. I thoroughly recommend it.'

The Revd Graham Carter, former President of the Methodist Conference

'Caring for others is in essence simply an expression of love for others and is therefore the task of every Christian. However, the reality is that some are more gifted than others in caring for those in need of pastoral care. Hence the development in many churches of pastoral teams whose task is to work alongside the leader/minister of the church in caring for people experiencing problems and challenges of one kind or another. For new and, indeed, seasoned members of such pastoral teams, *Pastoral Care in Practice* will prove to be a real boon. One great advantage that this book has over similar books on pastoral care is that although the author is a minister of the United Reformed Church, this guide has not been written within the context of one denomination or 'stream', but rather is immediately applicable to any expression of church. Michael Hopkins is to be congratulated on producing such an excellent guide to pastoral care.'

The Revd Dr Paul Beasley-Murray,
former Principal of Spurgeon's College

Pastoral Care
in Practice

Michael Hopkins

CANTERBURY PRESS
Norwich

© Michael Hopkins 2023

First published in 2023 by the Canterbury Press Norwich
Editorial office
3rd Floor, Invicta House
108–114 Golden Lane
London EC1Y 0TG, UK

www.canterburypress.co.uk

Canterbury Press is an imprint of Hymns Ancient & Modern Ltd
(a registered charity)

Hymns Ancient & Modern® is a registered trademark of
Hymns Ancient & Modern Ltd
13A Hellesdon Park Road, Norwich,
Norfolk NR6 5DR, UK

All rights reserved. No part of this publication may be reproduced,
stored in a retrieval system, or transmitted,
in any form or by any means, electronic, mechanical,
photocopying or otherwise, without the prior permission of
the publisher, Canterbury Press.

The Author has asserted his right under the Copyright, Designs and
Patents Act 1988 to be identified as the Author of this Work

Scripture quotations are from New Revised Standard Version
Bible: Anglicized Edition, copyright © 1989, 1995 National
Council of the Churches of Christ in the United States of America.
Used by permission. All rights reserved worldwide.

British Library Cataloguing in Publication data

A catalogue record for this book is available
from the British Library

978 1 78622 500 9

Typeset by Regent Typesetting

Contents

Foreword by the Rt Revd Dr Christopher Herbert ix
Introduction xi

1. Calling 1
2. Self-care 4
3. What is pastoral care? 10
4. Keeping everyone safe 15
5. Understanding people 20
6. Prayer 36
7. What is a 'visit'? 46
8. Caring for families and children 54
9. Caring for sick people 65
10. Caring in difficult situations 78
11. A reflection 88

Suggestions for further reading 93
Index of Bible References 95
Index of Names and Subjects 97

To my wife Rosie and daughter Joanna,
without whose love, support and encouragement
I could do very little; and to the churches that
I have tried to serve, and from whom I have learned
more than words can say.

Foreword

by the Rt Revd Dr Christopher Herbert

This is a wise, sensitive and very important book.

Drawing on his long and rich experience as a minister in the United Reformed Church, with characteristic generosity of heart and mind, Michael Hopkins outlines what he regards as the necessary foundations of good pastoral care. He speaks of the continuous love that God has for humanity and explores the biblical roots of pastoral care as seen in the life and teachings of Christ. From those two underlying realities, he gently concludes that healthy churches should be engaged in thoughtful consideration of what constitutes good pastoral care.

This, thank goodness, is not a 'shouty' book. It does not lay down hard guidelines that all churches should follow; rather, using questions and carefully chosen practical examples, it encourages the reader to think through (and pray about) the pastoral implications of the Christian faith. And from a practical perspective, it also outlines the legal, safeguarding and other elements of our cultural context which are the proper boundaries within which pastoral care can be offered. Further, each chapter concludes with questions that would provoke lively discussion in any church assessing its pastoral work, and that should be every church, shouldn't it?

For all those who are newly setting out on the path of pastoral care, whether lay or ordained, and for those who have been exercising a pastoral ministry for some time, it provides stimulating, challenging and encouraging insights.

PASTORAL CARE IN PRACTICE

I commend this book most warmly, believing it provides a long overdue recognition that pastoral care is one of the essential marks and gifts of Christian ministry.

+ *Christopher Herbert*
former Bishop of St Albans

Introduction

I have not written this book because I see myself as any kind of expert on pastoral care, far from it. I have written this book because I want to do better myself, and I want to encourage others to do better.

I first saw pastoral care being offered by my father, the Revd Derek Hopkins, in his work as a minister of the United Reformed Church. I am sure that laid foundations in me. I have received pastoral care from countless people, lay and ordained, in myriad ways. I was taught pastoral care by the Revd Dr Susan Durber, the Revd Dr Catherine Middleton and the Revd Tony Tucker while training for the ministry, and their teaching, built upon by twenty years' experience in pastoral charge, has developed my enthusiasm for pastoral care.

As a minister I am acutely aware that pastoral care is somewhat variable, and this is understandable in the mix of pressures upon churches and ministers today. However, assiduous pastoral care is still an essential tool in church life and mission. If we cannot care for the people that we do have, how can we recruit new members, and why would anyone want to join a church that didn't care?

Without the patient and tolerant support of everyone to whom I have ministered, it would not have been possible to do even what I have managed. I owe a particular debt of gratitude to the late Revd Graham Long, who was my minister for a time. Over thirty years ago he published a book, *Thank God You've Come*, for United Reformed Church Elders to learn about their ministry of pastoral care. Graham's pastoral work, renowned far and wide, and that book, are an important inspiration to me. In some ways this book might be an updated edition of Graham's, because the shape of the world and the church, and the parameters within which we minister, have changed beyond recognition since the 1980s. However, I also went further in writing a non-denominational book, so that as many people as possible have the potential to read, learn and use the book, and to develop their own skills in offering pastoral care.

Michael Hopkins
February 2023

I

Calling

Pastoral care is about making sure that people feel that they are known and loved, both by God and by their fellow members in the church. A healthy church is a church in which people know that they are loved, contact between members is welcome, and everyone is valued and feels safe. Pastoral care, both at times of crisis and in everyday life, is therefore an active proclamation of God's love in Christ for all the world.

Pastoral care is something that both clergy and lay people find themselves offering, because it is part of what it means to be Christian. Clergy generally receive more training than lay people, and their work is sometimes more formal, and in that sense the pastoral care they offer might be considered 'professional'. Many lay people may also have received significant training and/or bring wide experience, and in that sense can offer equally effective pastoral care. Indeed, at its heart pastoral care is about relationship expressing the love of God for someone, and so transcends the divisions between clergy and lay which are found in some churches.

Pastoral care might include:

- listening
- comforting
- encouraging
- offering practical help
- praying.

Pastoral care might involve:

- celebrating the joys of life
- supporting people, either through a prolonged difficulty or an immediate need
- considering the possibility of reconciliation with God, oneself and with others
- suggesting other sources of support, or offering a different perspective.

Pastoral care could be offered formally by a pastoral care team, network or church leaders, or informally in everyday relationships by individuals and/or small groups. Pastoral care might be both within and beyond the church.

The basis for pastoral care is found in the New Testament, as is the basis for all the ministries of the universal church. Pastoral care is about encouraging people to be and to do the best that God desires for them. A classic text for this is found in the first letter of Peter when he writes:

> But you are a chosen race, a royal priesthood, a holy nation, God's own people, in order that you may proclaim the mighty acts of him who called you out of darkness into his marvellous light. Once you were not a people, but now you are God's people; once you had not received mercy, but now you have received mercy. (1 Peter 2.9–10)

Peter's poetic words may not be an instruction manual for our age, but they are very obviously an encouragement that pastoral care is about helping each person to work out what it is that God wants them to be and to do, which is what being God's people means. Throughout the letters of the New Testament, the authors (Paul or whoever) give numerous examples of challenge and encouragement. Many of the moral and ethical strictures may sound uncomfortable or irrelevant to our twenty-first-century ears, yet all of them point to God's purpose set out in the letter to the Ephesians that 'speaking the truth in love, we must grow up in every way into him who is the head, into Christ (Ephesians 4.15), and also in the letter to the Galatians that 'Christ is formed in you' (Galatians 4.19).

The work of pastoral care has been at root the same throughout the history of church, even though it has been understood and expressed in different ways in different ages, which is to try to recognize what God is doing in people's lives and to encourage that. Whether we are exercising pastoral care as part of a formal ministry or not, whether we have much training or experience, or whether we are just starting out, our pastoral care of others can only be effective when we are able to recognize that God is also at work in us and in the world, as Paul puts it in his letter to the Philippians: 'I am confident of this, that the one who began a good work among you will bring it to completion by the day of Jesus Christ' (Philippians 1.6).

Some questions for personal reflection, or discussion with others

- To what extent do you feel a sense of calling towards offering pastoral care, doing a job that needs to be done, or some mixture of the two?

- Do any of the passages from the Bible speak to you in exploring the possibility of offering pastoral care?

- Where do you find encouragement in exploring the possibility of offering pastoral care?

A prayer to use

Loving God, you renew the strength of all who wait upon you. Support us with your Spirit, as we offer pastoral care to your people, and in your name; through Jesus Christ. Amen.

2

Self-care

Our pastoral care can only be as effective as it might be if we look after ourselves. This means that we need to consider our strengths, and where we might look for support when we need it.

Time

I know of no churches where most of the members have lots of spare time looking for things to do. There will always be some individuals who do have time, but many people involved in churches have demands of family, home life, other interests, and some are of working age. It is not unusual in churches to hear the words 'Given the time, I'd love to ...', yet, time after time, another phrase can also be heard in church life, 'I don't know how they find the time to do it all.'

Finding time is never easy, but in the end it comes down to the question of how we choose to spend it. What roles and tasks do we feel called to do? Which roles and tasks do we do because we feel that no one else will, or about which we feel a sense of guilt? A difficulty in many churches is that it can seem as if an ever-decreasing number of people getting older are trying to do the same things that more people and younger people once did. Especially at this point, there is a grave danger that we might lose sight of God and lose touch with God's calling. Throughout the Bible God calls all kinds and types of people in all manner of different situations to serve him, and the most common response to that call is one of utter astonishment, 'Who am I, God, that you should ask me?'

Most of us tend to use the standards of the world today when we consider what might be useful or worthwhile, but the Bible tells us time after time that the people God calls are very often the ones that worldly judgement has dismissed as of no account. This is true of Jesus no less, who seemed useless to the world hanging on the cross on Good Friday. Any sense of inadequacy that we might feel needs to be considered in the knowledge that God calls us and takes us on with all our weaknesses. As Paul put it, 'For God's foolishness is wiser than human wisdom, and God's weakness is stronger than human strength' (1 Corinthians 1.25). God does not ask us to be perfect before we begin to serve. God knows we are not and cannot be perfect, and God takes us as we are, simply asking us to be open to the Holy Spirit so that God can work through us. Astonishing as it may seem, God calls people like you and me to service.

Support

If we accept God's call, however tentatively, we need to take seriously all opportunities for support. We cannot be of much use to others if we do not care for ourselves. Along with ourselves, it is also important not to neglect the proper care of any partner/spouse and family that we have. God would be most unlikely to call us to something that damaged a loving and committed relationship. This is just as important in the case of single people who may also have wider family, and/or choose to define some friendships in a family way.

Another important matter is considering who our successor will be. By this I do not mean the thought that we cannot see who our successor is to be, but that we are not trying to make ourselves permanently indispensable. It really doesn't matter that we don't know the name of who will succeed us. Even if we have done a job for several years, a vacancy or a different way of doing things might not be disastrous. Indeed, it might be that the church benefits from some space in order to work out what to do next. In the same way, while we might have suggestions to make, it is not our sole responsibility to find someone to do the work needed.

In all that we do for God, we do that best when we can maintain a living relationship with God. Everyone has times when this feels stronger and times when this feels weaker, but working with God is easier if we are seeking God. In terms of support, we might look for practical or emotional support with the work of pastoral care, or we might look for spiritual support, to help us remember that we are working not in our own strength, but with the help of God.

Our offering

We offer a gift of time

We offer a gift of time, because pastoral care takes time. Developing and maintaining relationships with people takes time. For many of us, time is a premium commodity, which means that we need to plan its use very carefully.

We offer a gift of skills

We are called to pastoral care because others have discerned certain skills and gifts in us. Like all skills and gifts, they need to be drawn out and developed if their full potential is to be reached. Each person has vastly different skills and gifts, but together they make a team. Sometimes people think that pastoral care is only about spiritual things, but very often practical skills are an important part of the mix. Taking a home-cooked meal to someone, simply making a cup of tea, or a spare heater when their boiler is broken, often counts for far more than offering to pray for someone. Most of us sometimes feel inadequate, but what we are able to offer will almost certainly be sufficient.

'I wonder if you could do with ...' is often the lead into the offering of a gift in kind. At the height of the fruit and vegetable season, for instance, it is so easy to kill that kindness by responding with 'Our own plants are absolutely loaded this year. We just don't know what to do with all the stuff!' It is surely far better to try to find some way that doesn't stifle the instinct to give. We need to encourage kindness, not nip it in the bud! As we get to know people we may be able to redirect kindness that we find overwhelming. We could, for example, introduce the idea of giving to other people in the congregation, the more so if we can suggest individuals who would be blessed by a gift.

We offer a gift of ourselves

Sometimes we may use phrases such as 'I had a few minutes to spare so I thought I'd pop in.' Of course, it is meant with kindness, but might give the message that 'I haven't really got time for you.' If we say that we can't be in touch on Friday because that's our day off, it suggests that the relationship is purely professional, whereas to say that Friday happens not to be convenient, but might Thursday work for you is a little more sensitive. Everyone knows that we all need time to rest, but how we say it makes a difference.

We offer a gift of openness

We need to be open to those in our care. Of course, we shouldn't bare our soul in anguish every time we visit, but we do need to give enough of ourselves to satisfy their genuine concern for our well-being. Pastoral care will never succeed if people end up saying they never got to know us. Pastoral relationships, in some sense, embody what the psalmist calls the God who 'will neither slumber nor sleep' (Psalm 121.4), the God who gives himself to his people.

Receiving

We receive the gift of trust

Even the act of being invited into a person's home is a sign of some degree of trust. The more a relationship develops, the more trust should grow. Of course, we must never abuse that trust, of which more later.

We receive the gift of burdens

When people trust those who care about them they begin to share the things that burden them. Sharing burdens is a mark of a developing relationship. As the old adage says, a problem shared is a problem halved. Simply being willing to accept someone else's troubles can make all the difference to them. It can also make a world of difference for us if we accept their burden as something to be carried. This means that everyone who cares for others needs their own support mechanism of some kind. If we feel pressure mounting up on us, we need to feel able to ask for help.

We receive the gift of kindness

The overwhelming majority of the people we have to do with will want to be kind to us. This will show itself in a hospitable welcome, in genuine concern for our well-being, and perhaps the actual presentation of gifts.

We receive the gift of hospitable welcome by accepting it. It's unhelpful always to hover on the doorstep saying, 'I'd rather not come in, thanks all the same', unless we happen to be full of a cold but need to call. Nor is it helpful to launch into a protracted conversation on the doorstep or, for that matter, in the garden or in the street where neighbours and strangers might overhear. And we shouldn't feel we always have to take a gift in acknowledgement if we receive hospitality.

It will be helpful also to try to channel the kindness of some of the people for whom we care into the most creative form that it can take. Prayer is a very practical form of caring and it is wise to ask a few of those whom we know to have a kindly and generous spirit to commit themselves to pray for us personally. This itself may open up further opportunities for giving and receiving within the relationship.

Finally, but not least, we should always be on the lookout for the opportunity to 'grow' the next generation of those offering pastoral care.

Some questions for personal reflection, or discussion with others

- Where do you see your personal offering of time, and how God fits into that?
- Where do you see yourself having gifts to give?
- Where do you see yourself being able to receive gifts?

A prayer to use

Living God, even when we have known deep grief or raw emotion, you draw us back to you and you guide our ways through difficult days. Where our confidence or hope is dented, touch us with your love and remind us of how you understand. We pray in the name of Jesus. Amen.

3

What is pastoral care?

Pastoral care today is the same essential work, but the expression of it now takes many forms. All churches, of whatever denomination, have a responsibility to ensure the pastoral care of the congregation, and everyone has a part to play in this work, but some will have a larger responsibility. There is a wide variety of ways that this is expressed in churches of the same denomination or tradition, let alone the differences between denominations. Whatever the patterns, structures or traditions, the basic question is always: what is it that we are trying to do when we set out to care pastorally for people?

There are many different approaches that we can take to answer this question. The Bible has much to offer about pastoral care, not least the title used by Jesus: the Good Shepherd. Another approach is to remember that Jesus knew the Ten Commandments, and then added one in his own name: 'I give you a new commandment, that you love one another. Just as I have loved you, you also should love one another' (John 13.34). That was the instruction that Jesus gave to his disciples immediately after he had washed their feet. Offering pastoral care is surely trying to apply that new commandment through the life of the church.

Trying to apply that new commandment means that we can look to Jesus to find both the purpose and the approach of our pastoral care. The words 'as I have loved you' are the crux of the matter, and our inspiration. The challenge to us is to do our best to try to embody those words in the life of the church as we offer pastoral care. Applying that new commandment also means remembering the context. The Ten Commandments were given at a particular time and place, in the context of the

WHAT IS PASTORAL CARE?

freedom from slavery in Egypt that God had granted God's people. And likewise the new commandment given by Jesus shapes the culture and ethos of what church in general, and pastoral care in particular, means: 'By this everyone will know that you are my disciples, if you have love for one another' (John 13.35). If we take this at all seriously, then care for each other in the church is neither an optional extra nor a secondary matter, because it belongs to the essential nature of the church. Naturally, Jesus was thinking of the church, and that is where pastoral care begins, but it doesn't have to be where pastoral care ends. Inevitably in a living and active church, pastoral care spills over into the surrounding community.

There is no universal pattern of pastoral care. What is suitable for a large growing charismatic congregation in a city centre is unlikely to work in a small village church; what is suitable for a Roman Catholic church may not be as suitable in a Baptist church. What is useful if there is a full-time resident minister in one church may not work in a rural group of many small churches. What works where the leaders of a church are long-term residents in the community may meet difficulties in a city-centre church with a transient membership and leadership.

For pastoral care to have any chance of success, it is essential for a church to work out together the pattern best suited to their local situation. Here are some suggestions to bear in mind while working that out.

1 Pastoral care does not always equal visiting. Visiting is part of pastoral care but is not an end in itself. Some approaches to visiting are simply a waste of time. Others can be like gold-dust. When properly conducted, visiting is a valuable arm of pastoral care, but pastoral care that is merely limited to visiting is a poor thing indeed. More will be said about 'visiting' later on.

2 If pastoral care is to achieve its greatest potential, it will need to encompass prayer, 'visiting', giving, and receiving. These are things that we see in the ministry of Jesus, as examples of basic pastoral activities.

3 While pastoral care needs to be shaped carefully to meet the particular needs of each church, it is important to remember that a great deal of informal and often spontaneous caring goes on in every community. A full understanding of pastoral care will include encouraging this informal caring within each congregation.

One reason that the early church made a major impact in the ancient world was not because it was good at organizing but because Christians were good at caring. It was said, 'How these Christians love one another.'

Putting this into practice relies upon three Cs: care, communication and commitment. Whatever structure is used locally to manage the pastoral care of the congregation, pastoral care at its best contains a three-fold emphasis:

Care: by this we mean love showing itself in action. John says, 'We love because God first loved us' (1 John 4.19). Pastoral care is both our response to God's love by trying to offer that love to others, and our actions as people through whom God is working as God cares for others. People will only know that God cares for them when they know what it is to be cared for.

Communication: in basic terms this means 'keeping people in touch'. Personal contact is itself one way of showing that God loves people as individuals and cares for them personally. God cares for each person because to God each person is beloved, precious and unique. Pastoral care is how that loving, caring relationship is made known. Even the relatively mundane activity of 'keeping people in touch' says something about how their importance is valued, by the person offering them pastoral care, by the church and by God. They are God's children.

Commitment: the point of pastoral care is, as Paul puts it, 'to bring each one into God's presence as a mature individual in union with Christ' (Colossians 1.28). Challenging as this may sound, this is the goal of pastoral care. Our aspiration, our

WHAT IS PASTORAL CARE?

hope and all that we work for is that every member of the congregation should be a full part of the body of Christ, taking their full share of life in Christ.

Perhaps it is not surprising that the quality of the pastoral care offered is a key factor in the health of churches, and healthy churches are more likely to be growing numerically. Surely it is reasonable to expect that where people are befriended and supported, where they are cared for, prayed for and prayed with, and surrounded by a warm-hearted fellowship where love and respect for them abound, hearts will be moved in response and commitment will grow.

The primary purpose of this book is to help those who are new to offering pastoral care, but, hopefully, it will be of help also to those who have had previous experience of offering pastoral care, and those who offer training and support to those offering pastoral care. There are three points which will help pastoral care to be as effective as it can be:

1 Reading, exploration and learning can help us to develop relationships but can never replace genuine concern, care and affection, which are at the heart of all good relationships. Tools can help us make more effective those qualities in relationships which encourage people and build them up.

2 We can learn to foster more perceptive relationships, but as relationships develop we must avoid judging people. In pastoral relationships it is all too easy to become judgemental, but if that happens supportive relationships become almost impossible. If we are standing in judgement, we are standing at a distance. Judgementalism takes us away from people rather than closer to them.

3 We must keep appropriate confidentiality. Apart from where someone expresses a wish to harm themselves or someone else, or discloses abuse, if we feel the need to share something we have been told in confidence, we should seek permission

before doing so. This may mean that sometimes we have to hide a person's identity if we are requesting prayer support for them. It will almost certainly mean that from time to time we will possess unsettling knowledge that has been given to us in confidence.

Offering pastoral care means that we sometimes find ourselves in situations where we know something but have no apparent means of doing anything about it, and this can be very frustrating. The most practical thing we can do in such situations is to offer the matter to God, continuing to ask for God's blessing on the person involved and to give thanks that God will not withhold it. After that, we need to be prepared to take action when God opens the door to new possibilities, but try not to feel disappointed if it becomes clear that someone else must take that action. It is enough that our prayers have been answered and that God has blessed the one for whom we have been concerned.

Some questions for personal reflection, or discussion with others

- How does 'love one another as I have loved you' fit into your own experiences of pastoral care?
- Does your church have a pattern or system for pastoral care, and where do you fit into it?
- How do you see yourself and the three Cs?

A prayer to use

Risen Christ, at Easter you showed us that your love was too strong even for death, but only once all seemed at its worst. Through your risen life today, help us to offer your love, never despair, and remember that you always offer hope. Amen.

4

Keeping everyone safe

Safeguarding is an essential component of church life today, and rightly so. It is not possible in a book of this kind either to replicate or to summarize different denominational safeguarding policies. It simply can not do that because safeguarding policies are continually developing. Everyone involved in pastoral care needs to avail themselves of the appropriate checks required[1] and safeguarding training required by their denominations. This may seem an imposition and a lack of trust in us, but it is essential so that everyone can have confidence in us. Safeguarding is about keeping everyone safe, which means both the people we care for and ourselves, so we need have nothing to fear from it, and nor would it be helpful to resent it or try to get around it. What this chapter does is to set out the general principles, as they are at the time of writing, underlying safeguarding, and seek to set all pastoral care in a safeguarding context.

All safeguarding is guided by the foundations of the gospel, human rights, and international and national law. Safeguarding is about enabling everyone in the church to support fully the personal dignity and rights of all children, young people and adults, as enshrined in the Human Rights Act 1998 (UK) and the 1989 United Nations Convention on the Rights of the Child. All safeguarding work is undertaken within the law of the land and associated government guidance, which sets out a range of safeguarding duties and responsibilities. Legal arrangements and requirements vary between jurisdictions.

---

1 At the time of writing, in England and Wales a DBS check, and membership of the PVG scheme in Scotland.

There has been widespread coverage in the media of the failure of various organizations and individuals adequately to prevent, and protect children from, abuse, including many high-profile cases. Sadly, sometimes churches have made the same mistakes as other institutions. In recent years, there has also been a growing understanding of the importance of recognizing abuse against adults who are vulnerable, whether inflicted deliberately or as a consequence of neglect. There now exists a generous spread of legislation, guidance, research and reports from all sectors. This has led to the development of safeguarding policies and procedures. Closer working partnerships have been forged between safeguarding for both children and adults at risk. There has also been a growing commitment among all those who work with vulnerable groups to improve working practices.

All churches intend to value every human being as part of God's creation and the whole people of God. At the heart of the church is a deep sense of a place of welcome, hospitality and openness, which demonstrates the nature of God's grace and love for all. All churches are called to be places where the transformational love of God is embodied, and the gift of life in all its fullness is offered to all people. Putting this into practice means that there be no distinctions of gender, race, disability, sexual orientation, religion/beliefs, pregnancy/maternity and gender reassignment. Everyone has the right to protection from abuse and not to be treated less favourably than others, irrespective of any personal or protected characteristic.

Safeguarding is about actions which the church takes to promote safety for everyone. This means that everyone involved in giving pastoral care needs to: promote the welfare of children, young people and adults; work to prevent abuse from occurring; and seek to protect and to respond well to those who have been abused.

Where someone may pose a risk to others, safeguarding policies will contain ways to deal with that risk. Safeguarding is a shared responsibility, so everyone associated with the church who comes into contact with children, young people and adults who may be vulnerable has a role to play, supported by consistent policies promoting good practice. Everyone in the church, not just those involved in pastoral care, has a part to play in maintaining a safer environment.

Based on these foundations, churches now have a clear duty to promote a safer environment and culture; safely recruit and support all those with any responsibility for children and adults within the church; respond promptly and appropriately to every safeguarding concern or allegation; care pastorally for victims and survivors of abuse and other people who have been affected; care pastorally for those who are the subject of concerns of allegations of abuse and others who have been affected; carry out risk assessments and put safeguarding measures in place where individuals pose a present risk to children, young people, or vulnerable adults. This all sounds very daunting, but current safeguarding training and current safeguarding policies, procedures and guidance equip us to play our part in this bigger picture.

What does a safe church look like?

Some churches will give a strong impression that everything is wonderful, sometimes to the extent that one might think they are suggesting that God's kingdom has been fulfilled. A more honest approach is seen in churches which also own properly, while not being bogged down by, issues of brokenness, of failure, sin and disappointment, including being expressed through church leaders who are secure enough to be honest and vulnerable.

Safe churches have communications which are a genuine dialogue between all people, showing appropriate respect for everyone, and where there is encouragement, indeed welcoming, of different perspectives and views. It should not feel that people are taking a risk by expressing different views to other members of the church.

Safe churches do not contain coercive and/or controlling behaviours, and do not have a command and control style of leadership. Poor behaviour, such as bullying, is challenged and resolved when it occurs. The responsibility to address difficult situations is not evaded, and all involved in the church support each other through difficult times.

In safe churches power is shared and distributed instead of being vested in a few people. This means that leadership styles become inclusive and consultative, rather than controlling, and there are no powerful elites or cliques dominating the life and affairs of the church. It also means that safe boundaries between people are understood and observed, and that no one is isolated or left out of the church's life and activities.

Safe churches practise self-reflection. By this I mean that both collectively and as individuals, without becoming trapped in navel-gazing, the church spends time reflecting on their behaviours and relationships. By doing this, people learn to be more aware of the impact they can have on others, any tendency towards, and dangers of, clerical deference are acknowledged and actively guarded against, and feedback from others is welcomed. Leaders in the church learn from failures and reviews, and so take appropriate actions to seek to prevent any recurrence.

In safe churches, the importance of protecting people's personal data and privacy is understood, so that everyone should feel safe in sharing relevant personal information because they know their privacy is taken seriously. In the same way, people know how information about them will be used and they can trust people to use it appropriately.

Having the attitudes, behaviours and ethos of a safe church needs to be developed consciously and purposefully, and to be nurtured and reviewed. It might sometimes feel daunting, but we all need to start somewhere. Pastoral care is not about solving all the problems of the church ourselves, still less about seeking to take over God's role in that, but it is about learning the part we play within that work, and always ensuring that our care for others is safe, our care for ourselves is safe, and our care for the whole church is safe. If each of us take our part, being a safe church is not a difficult task.

Some questions for personal reflection, or discussion with others

- Do you feel that your church is generally a safe church?
- How do you feel safeguarding interacts with and impacts upon pastoral care?
- What have you learned from safeguarding training which influences pastoral care?

A prayer to use

God who is love, help our church, through each one of us, to be a place where everyone is both welcome and safe. Keep us compassionate and kind, but also watchful and ready to ask questions, so that everyone in your church may be safe; through Jesus Christ our Lord. Amen.

5

Understanding people

Individuals, households and families come in all manner of shapes, sizes and combinations. In the past it was not unheard of for churches to operate on the basic assumption that the people they were attempting to serve and to recruit into membership were all straight white middle-class families. One minister, who was widowed and had a child, found it somewhat bemusing that someone led prayers for 'single mothers' in a tone that managed to convey both judgement and pity but no understanding. Another minister, originally from west Africa, was serving a church in a market town and was told by one church member that while she was a lovely minister it was a pity that she wasn't serving a church in London as 'there would be more people like you'. Perhaps churches have improved in this regard over the years, but if these are stories that clergy have encountered, how much more have church members, or potential church members who thought better of it, encountered? While doubtless unintended, micro-aggressions and prejudice have quietly harmed the pastoral care of countless churches for generations, and we can always do better.

Micro-aggressions are behaviours which say to an individual that they do not quite belong and are not welcome. These very often take the form of insensitive comments, questions or actions which undermine confidence, questioning the right to belong, subtle insults or criticism, and slights or insults often disguised as a joke or banter. People on the receiving end of these behaviours will usually feel uncomfortable or hurt.

The Equality Act (2010) creates what it terms 'protected characteristics'. For any of these protected characteristics, it is against the law to discriminate, harass or victimize people, and to offer any distinctions in employment or in the provision of goods or services. How the precise terms of the law apply to churches, or where there might be exemptions, is largely irrelevant in terms of pastoral care, because an appropriate Christian response in pastoral situations is always to do our best to include and accept everyone, and to do so as God made them, not as we wish they were. These protected characteristics are:

- age
- gender reassignment
- being married or in a civil partnership
- being pregnant or on maternity leave
- disability
- race including colour, nationality, ethnic or national origin
- religion or belief
- sex.

Equality does not mean that everybody is the same; rather, it is about recognizing that everybody is different, but at the same time should be treated with an equal level of respect. This means treating everyone in the same way, acknowledging and respecting differences and the needs that arise from that, so that no one is excluded, however inadvertently. If we are doing this properly, then we will not use stereotypes, and will understand where differences matter, such as people needing additional support or a different approach because of disadvantages that they face in life.

When we are able to see the many positive things about differences we can then recognize, respect and value differences. Appreciating this diversity helps us to recognize the contribution that each makes, and promotes dignity and respect. Treating other people as we wish to be treated is a good start, but we need to do more. We must treat others with empathy, and seek to understand their experience and their particular needs.

A first step on this journey is to understand our own identity as a combination of different parts and layers, all of which are known and loved by God. We need to recognize that not everyone has had the same life chances and opportunities, and some may need help and support to be able to take advantage of the opportunities which others may not even have realized were advantages. Some people have faced discrimination or disadvantage, and been excluded, while others have had privileges that they may not even be aware of.

In order to offer effective pastoral care to people, we and our churches need to learn to value every human being as part of God's creation and the whole people of God. Pastoral care relies upon each church being a place of deep welcome, serious hospitality and genuine openness, demonstrating the nature of God's grace and love for all. Pastoral care means helping churches to be places where the transformational love of God is embodied, and life in all its fullness is a gift that is offered to all people. This does not mean there are no boundaries or limits to the church's inclusivity and hospitality. Boundaries exist in the church to enable it to remain faithful to being the Body of Christ, and seeking to be a safe space for those who participate in its communal life. God loves all people, and pastoral care means seeking to live out that love in every part of church life.

Language

Our use of language matters. Jesus asked people that he met what it was they wanted from him, and we do best at language when we engage other people in a conversation about what terms or language are most acceptable and helpful to them. Not every member of a group will want to be described in the same way, so it is important to listen to how people identify themselves, and to be aware of how language evolves. For example, some people wish specific pronouns to be used, and common courtesy dictates that we refer to people as they wish to be known regardless of our own views. As another example, I used to understand that BAME was a term that was preferred by black, Asian and minority ethnic people to describe themselves, but I now know that not everyone likes this term and some people prefer to be known as people from the Global Majority.

Bias

Every one of us has what are sometimes called unconscious or affinity biases. This is a normal part of how our brains work, and is simply a part of our natural people preferences. Whatever you call it, our biases are often about what we are drawn to, rather than what we reject. Each of us naturally has a better understanding of people who are like us and of familiar situations. This means that people who look like us, sound like us and share our interests are easier to relate to and identify with. As we meet, socialize and encounter people beyond what is familiar and comfortable to us, we come across new experiences and ideas, diverse people and different ways of expressing our emotions and thoughts. Sometimes this helps us to appreciate difference, but sometimes it can reinforce our innate concerns.

Sometimes our biases and affinities are rooted deeply in our subconscious, and we can find ourselves making decisions which bypass our normal, rational and logical thinking without even knowing that we are doing this. This can be exacerbated when we are under stress or anxious, or if we find ourselves needing to make decisions on the spur of the moment. This means that our minds can sometimes take us to the very brink of bias and poor decision making without us even knowing it.

However, our brains are constantly learning and adapting, and while deep-rooted biases, and even prejudices, may still be in the back of our minds, we can learn to challenge those biases and prejudices. Our brains have a mechanism to control bias and prevent it becoming behaviour. For this to happen, our brains need to see a mismatch between our instinctive people preferences and our wider goals, by which I mean that if we have personal goals that are fair, moral and value-driven this can help us not to follow our natural bias. Being aware of our biases and how strong they are can then help us to manage them better, which helps other people as well as us, and so improves the pastoral care that we can offer.

Age

If we look back to the middle of the twentieth century, people's life expectancy was much shorter than it is now. Children were expected to be seen and not heard, the term teenager was little known, and several generations of a family living together was a normal practice. Many churches have seen a decline in the numbers of younger people generally, and young families in particular, regularly attending their services. Sometimes people speak of a missing generation. Modern life, technology and working patterns have a very significant impact on both families and churches, which brings both opportunities and challenges.

Any church that wants to include everyone needs to be committed to the full participation of all age groups, and to using each person's skills and talents. Sadly, the reality does not always match this aim, often because some people make age-related assumptions, or the traditional ways of churches going about things simply do not meet the need of different generations today. Offering effective pastoral care means that we need to work hard to include both young and old.

Poverty

Social justice has been a feature of church life for centuries. From Tudor times until the nineteenth century, the Church of England administered the entirety of what is now known as the welfare state through parishes. In the eighteenth, nineteenth and twentieth centuries many churches, especially nonconformist churches, were deeply concerned with social justice and seeking to improve the lives of the poor.

Public perceptions of poverty are often very different now from the reality. In the UK, 80% of the population believe that large numbers of people falsely claim benefits, but the real figure is 0.9%. Over 50% of people in Britain believe that benefits are too high, but since 1979, benefit levels have halved relative to the average wage. Some 60% of the UK public say that the poor could cope if they handled their money correctly, but an unemployed person over 25 will receive 40% of the amount calculated by the Joseph Rowntree foundation as necessary for a minimum income, while a couple with two children will get 60% of what they need. All evidence shows that people living on benefits manage their money very carefully indeed. Parents being unwilling to work is the most commonly cited cause of UK child poverty among both churchgoers and the general public, but the majority of working-age households in poverty are in employment, and 1.4 million of these work fewer hours than they would wish, moving in and out of low-paid and insecure jobs. Addiction to drink and drugs is the second most commonly cited cause, but less than 4% of people on benefits report any kind of addiction.[1]

Over 14 million people in the UK live in poverty today. Of those who are of working age over half are in households that are working. Poverty means that these people struggle to provide the basics for their families, and are hindered from participating in normal social life. As a people trying to offer pastoral care, we need to understand that people should have sufficient material resources to live with dignity and to realize their God-given potential. Human dignity requires more than simply meeting the minimum bodily needs of food, hygiene and shelter. Dignity requires sufficient resources to be able to be a part of a wider society, and for children to be able to develop and have opportunities that society affords other children.

Is it poverty when a 17-year-old can never afford to go to a disco? Is it poverty if you can only afford the cheapest things? Poverty is about more than shortage of money, because it

---

[1] Statistics reported by the Joint Public Issues Team in 2013, https://www.jointpublicissues.org.uk/wp-content/uploads/Truth-And-Lies-Report-smaller.pdf (accessed 11.4.23)

encompasses rights and relationships, how people are treated and how they regard themselves, powerlessness, exclusion and loss of equity. Is poverty having no say in decisions that affect your community, but seeing regeneration imposed from outside by companies and councils? Is poverty not just experiencing these issues once in a while, but facing them every single day? Is poverty going without a winter coat yourself so you can afford them for your children? Is poverty having to decide whether to eat a meal or heat your house?

There are 14.4 million people who experience poverty in the UK – that is over 1 in 5. The younger you are, the more likely you are to experience poverty. There are 4.5 million children who experience poverty – that is 1 in 3 children. Most families experiencing poverty are in paid work. Some 3.6 million children in working families experience poverty; 14% of children in families with two full-time working parents experience poverty.[2]

How do we respond to this as we try to offer pastoral care? Luke says, 'The Spirit of the Lord is upon me, because he has anointed me to bring good news to the poor. He has sent me to proclaim release to the captives and recovery of sight to the blind, to let the oppressed go free, to proclaim the year of the Lord's favour' (Luke 4.18–19).

If we are to offer effective pastoral care to people in poverty, we must challenge the assumptions that we and our churches make about poverty and class. Poverty is more than just a lack of resources: it affects how people feel about themselves and how others see them. Reaching out to poor people, trying to be a church where people of all classes and backgrounds are equal, is a vital part of how we respond in pastoral care to people in poverty. Some of our habitual ways of doing things, such as the time of day that we hold meetings and the way we present written papers, do not work for some people from disadvantaged backgrounds.

---

2 Figures from the Social Metrics Commission, 2020, https://socialmetricscommission.org.uk/wp-content/uploads/2020/06/Measuring-Poverty-2020-Web.pdf (accessed 11.4.23).

Disability

Someone with a disability is anyone who has a physical or mental impairment which is substantial and has a long-term adverse effect on their ability to carry out normal day-to-day activities. It is also important to remember that anyone may be temporarily disabled, for example when recovering from a serious illness or accident. Many people with disabilities feel that their impairments are not what disables them, because it is the built environment that is not planned with their needs in mind, or the attitudes of other people, which disables them. Disabilities can be sensory impairment, such as hearing or eyesight; mobility or dexterity impairment; neurological conditions (that is, damage or limitation in the nervous system or brain); learning disabilities, which means substantial and life-long limitations to mental or cognitive abilities which are life-long; learning difficulties, which tend to affect people in only some areas of their lives and do not affect their intellectual ability; mental health problems; and long-term limiting illness, which means any health condition that limits day-to-day activities over a long period and or that can recur frequently. This list is not exhaustive, and care should be taken not to put people into categories. It is vital to remember that many disabilities and impairments cannot be seen.

Many people with disabilities and impairments feel they have to fight for what others take for granted; they do not speak up about their needs because they have experienced others not listening to or considering their issues. Many people with disabilities and impairments feel disempowered, not because of their impairments but because of outdated systems and practices, inflexible environments and other people's negative attitudes. If we are offering pastoral care to disabled people it is essential that we listen to them. If we listen, we then need to respond to what we hear by adjusting how things are done. Some adjustments can be made quickly and easily by individuals changing their behaviour, but other adjustments may require more investment of time, energy and resources.

What could our church do to make it a more inclusive place where all can be heard and feel welcome? In what ways could we challenge assumptions about disability? What do we mean by normal? Is 'normal' an exclusive club? What could we do to ensure that the financial cost of making our church accessible is planned for?

Sex and gender

Sex and gender are spoken of much, but what do they mean? 'Sex' refers to the biological and physiological characteristics that define men and women. 'Gender' refers to the socially constructed roles, behaviours, activities and attributes that a given society considers appropriate for men and women. Put simply, 'sex' is about our anatomy, and 'gender' is about how we express ourselves in terms of masculinity and femininity. Ideas of what is masculine and feminine vary a great deal from society to society, within societies and even from person to person. This means that people cannot just be defined by their sex. We also need to remember that some people have the physical characteristics of both male and female, and there are people who identify as transgender. Transgender refers to someone who had the anatomy of one sex at birth, which may be inconsistent with how they feel about their gender, or the gender of their brain. It is inaccurate to make assumptions about people's skills, aptitudes and preferences based on sex or gender. If we are offering pastoral care we need to recognize people for who they are, not who they are assumed to be because of their sex or gender. Many societies have developed to favour men and masculine behaviour, and as a consequence gender/sex discrimination is experienced disproportionately by women. Across the centuries, Christianity has assigned leadership and power privilege to men over women, and emphasized masculine imagery and language to describe God. There is more diverse language and imagery in the Bible, and there has been re-interpretation of specific texts that proscribe aspects of female speech and behaviour in relation to men and in church, but this needs to be followed through in practice.

What assumptions do we and our church have about leadership and gender? How does gender discrimination affect individuals and the mission of the church? Is there a particular culture of leadership in our church that promotes or inhibits gender equality? Are there gender-specific roles in our church? How can we ensure that roles are inclusive?

If we are to offer pastoral care safely to everyone, good leadership makes a difference in how people feel accepted and welcomed for all they are. Using gender-neutral language can help people to feel welcome, not least because no one can assume gender from appearance. We may be offering pastoral care to people who are trans or non-binary without being aware of it. When people are transitioning gender they often say that they are still the same person but are just being more real about being themselves. Many people need our help and support to cope with change. Transgender people are usually the best people to advise us on trans issues, but we must remember that it is unlawful to disclose that someone is transgender without their consent.

Race

Racial discrimination and assumptions about race and ethnicity affect people every day in their general life and in the life of the church. However, ethnic diversity in both churches and society can enrich both our personal and world views if we learn from other people's stories and are aware of the impact of racial discrimination. In Britain, White British people form 'the dominant group' and might not be aware of the issues that other ethnic groups face.

Assumptions that are made about people based on their race or national origin are often deeply set within our own cultural context, whatever culture we come from, and are often incorrect, which makes it all the more important to get to know people. All churches condemn racism, and while many desire racial justice, the reality for many people from Global Majority backgrounds is often negative and not affirming. Sadly, overt racism does still happen and needs to be challenged immediately. Assumptions about people based on their race, colour, ethnic or national origins are often unconsciously entrenched. People in the dominant group are often not aware of how this affects others. Really listening to people from the Global Majority is essential if racism is to be eliminated. Avoiding tokenism, while really listening and recognizing skills and talents, enriches all of us.

What is your experience of your church dealing with issues of differences in 'race' and culture? Is it right that a majority group or those who shout the loudest in churches make the decisions? How does racial discrimination impact on individuals and on the mission of churches? Is there a particular culture of leadership within churches that promotes or inhibits race equality? What could you and your church do to make it a more inclusive place where all can be heard and all are made to feel welcome? How might we encourage greater diversity? What are the processes for identifying and selecting new leaders in the church? Are they really open to everyone?

LGBTQIA+ people

Pastoral care is about creating safe and sacred spaces where everyone can encounter the infinite, unconditional, intimate love of God. Lesbian, Gay, Bisexual, Transgender, Queer or Questioning, Intersex, Asexual people, often known as LGBTQIA+ are an established part of the life and ministry of many, if not most, churches, whether people realize this or not. LGBTQIA+ people experience their sexual orientation as an authentic and integral part of their identity, but often face hostility from other people whose attitude to them is a barrier, and often feel invisible, isolated or unsupported in church because their identity as LGBTQIA+ people is often ignored or not acknowledged.

While we recognize a wide diversity in how Christians understand Scripture in relation to sexual orientation, offering pastoral care challenges us to acknowledge this diversity, to believe that Christ called us to strive to live together, to realize that this can only be done by reliance on the grace of God to enable mutual respect, love and continuing exploration together, to recognize that these views are held as deep convictions, to acknowledge that those who are called to Christ are done so through God's calling rather than personal choosing, and to agree to continue to explore these differences in the light, under the guidance of the Holy Spirit, through our pilgrimage of faith.

In offering pastoral care, we need to consider to what extent labels matter to God. How might our and our church's assumptions about LGBTQIA+ people impact on individuals and on our church's mission? What could we and our church do to recognize, affirm and celebrate LGBTQIA+ people in our church's life?

Refugees

Around the world there are almost countless wars and conflicts, many of which are fuelled by weapons constructed in and sold by countries in western Europe and other parts of the northern hemisphere. Many people are escaping this fighting, in fear for their lives, and sadly find much hostility where they seek sanctuary. People fleeing violence not only need shelter but also compassion. They are looking for words of comfort and support along with food and shelter. Some churches have developed a particular ministry to refugees in their community, and specialist training is available.

Working with people

Whoever we are offering pastoral care to, everyone is a person, loved and known by God. Whether they have particular factors to take account of, or not, we are seeking to offer each person the love of God through our pastoral care. We have been given the same basic equipment for developing relationships as anyone else: two eyes and two ears.

Seeing

By looking, we can learn a great deal about the people for whom we are trying to care. We can begin to build up a profile of each person. Is their garden filled with flowers, vegetables or weeds? Is their home filled with books, and if so what kind? Can we see signs that reveal someone's interests and tastes? Through them we build up a picture of what people are like. However, we should never make assumptions, because someone may hide their real person behind what others see. Someone who appears very flamboyant may in fact be a very timid person. Someone who seems to be solitary or a loner may actually be someone with a deep yearning for friendship who has been badly hurt. Can we avoid the phrase 'I presume'? Each time we use it, there will be a far greater number of times when it is an unspoken influence.

Listening

We also need to use our ears. We need to listen carefully to our people because sometimes listening to what someone does not say tells us more than what they do say. Someone whose conversation is always full of the cost of things may be telling us that they are financially hard pressed and could do with some extra help, while someone who never mentions financial needs may in fact be too proud to do so. When we listen carefully we might notice that people speak in different tones at different times, which gives us an indication of inner feelings and can often alert us to areas of real need and tell us too about someone's inner feelings. After a difficult meeting, someone once said to an old friend that they noticed that they still dropped their voice when they were angry.

However, we do well if we remember that we can never get to know someone completely. Our impression of them will always be provisional, but that is fine to begin with as we offer them pastoral care, start to pray for them, and relate to them in ways which express the interest and friendship of the church. As we do this we strengthen the affirmation of God's love for them in their lives. Even in its simplest form this is a spiritual ministry, as Paul prayed for the church in Ephesus that they might know 'the breadth and length and height and depth, and to know the love of Christ that surpasses knowledge, so that you may be filled with all the fullness of God' (Ephesians 3.18–19).

Balance

With two eyes, two ears and one mouth, the ratio of these parts provides us with a useful guide when we set out to develop our pastoral care. It has been said that we have two eyes, two ears and one mouth for good reason. With one eye we see people, and with the other we see what God has done and is doing; with one ear we are listening for God speaking, and with the other we hear what people are saying; and only when we have used our eyes and ears carefully should we speak.

It can be easy to feel we know what people's needs are, and therefore easy to get them wrong. Someone may be standing on the pavement looking somewhat helpless, but that does not necessarily mean that they want to cross the road. We need to take care to understand people's real needs.

Offering pastoral care is about encouraging people to be what they already are, the people of God. If we are seeking to encourage people, building them up in their Christian faith, and affirming that they are loved and valued for themselves, we need to convey that message plainly. We shall need to use our eyes and ears carefully. We shall need to identify and meet practical everyday needs which often enable us to convey the message without actually using the words: there is a great truth in the adage 'say it with flowers'. In the same way, offering some a lift to an event actually expresses their inclusion. However, saying 'it was the least I could do' might be taken that we weren't bothered to make any effort.

Friendship

God grants people spiritual gifts to be used, and friendship within a church is vitally important if these gifts are to be identified and developed. Through friendship God helps each person to fulfil their God-given potential, and releases their gifts into the community. Fostering friendships, then, is an important part of pastoral care. The more friendships that people make in their first six months in a church the more likely they are to go on to be leaders in the congregation in the future.

Sometimes we also need to read between the lines, looking for a reality that isn't actually made explicit. Listening and looking helps us to be discerning in our care for people, which is a most ancient gift of God. Some people have very particular needs, and if we do not share those needs, we are called to give special care and attention to understanding them. All people need our best listening and looking so that we put ourselves in the strongest position that we can to help them.

Some questions for personal reflection, or discussion with others

- Do you have a sense of your own biases?
- Do any of the minorities mentioned in this chapter strike a particular chord with you, or present you with a particular challenge?
- How do you feel about listening and looking twice as much as speaking?

A prayer to use

Loving God, help us to accept other people just as you accept each one of us. Help us to care for everyone, not just for people like us. Help us to care for people as they are, and as they may become. Help us where we need to change, and renew us with your Spirit; through Jesus Christ our Lord. Amen.

6

Prayer

An integral part of pastoral care, however we exercise it, is prayer, however we understand that. When should we pray? When is shared prayer the most appropriate response? How might we formulate prayers? What are the pitfalls to be aware of?

If pastoral care is to be successful, it needs to involve prayer, whatever we might understand by prayer. It is not too much to say that prayer is the key that opens the way to all things pastoral. Without prayer for people in our care we shall not care for them in the distinctive way our faith makes possible. Prayer marks the difference between a social club and a Christian fellowship. If the church is not a fellowship it is not a church.

Praying for people, even if we do not get to see them very often, is caring for them. Sometimes we may know of particular needs at a particular moment in time, such as sickness or bereavement, work difficulties, or a source of stress or anxiety. Sometimes we may see ongoing general needs – difficulty in making friendships, struggles over faith and worship, family anxieties, for example. Sometimes we may know so little about people that even the general situation offers little guidance.

This means that our prayers will vary in content and over time. If nothing else, it really is sufficient simply to remember a person by name or by face consciously in God's presence. There is no doubt that God can take such prayerful intentions and use them. If we pray for people we don't keep in touch with very much, we might find that we are prompted by God – that openings are made, perhaps the time is made available or an unknown opportunity appears, even in the busiest life, for us to be in touch with them. Quite how this happens may remain a mystery, but we can affirm that it does happen and that to offer prayers can make it possible. Contact and 'visiting' grows out of praying, and in this way the prayer becomes the really practical part.

When we encounter a prompting to be in touch with someone, we may find ourselves faced with some uncertainties or lack of confidence. If that happens, a good response is to pray for ourselves, perhaps a prayer like this:

> God, I don't really know this person, but I want to try to be a friend, so please help us both to prepare for friendship.

Neither should we forget what brought us to that person in the first place. If our presence there is a response to the prompting of God within us, then the way for our contact has been made ready. Even though we may feel inadequate, we can go with confidence and good courage.

It is obvious that a church whose leaders pray for those in their care will be the better for it, but it will be even better where the members of the church pray for each other. The apostle Paul taught his churches to do good to everyone 'and especially to those who belong to our family in the faith' (Galatians 6.10). Praying is the highest form of doing good, and we will always benefit from encouraging people to pray for each other. Sometimes we will know the people and the situation well enough to ask people to pray specifically for someone, but we should always take the greatest care to avoid this becoming gossip.

There are ways we can encourage people to pray for one another.

1 When we become aware of particular needs or concerns, we can ask permission for those to be included in the prayers during a service, or placed on a prayer list or similar. Permission must always be sought before any use of someone's name or any information at all about their situation is given, and then any conditions, or a refusal, must be respected.

Even when we cannot share a particular need with others, that does not prevent us praying privately for the situation that has been shared. The simple knowledge that we are praying can be a powerful help to those in need.

2 Some churches have developed ways of encouraging people to pray for each other as an organized part of their church life. Obviously, all of these require the same explicit consent as for including prayers in services etc. These might include things such as:

- arranging for a prayer request book/sheet to be available in the church
- circulating prayer requests on a notice sheet
- circulating prayer requests to named individuals who agreed to pray for particular requests
- dividing the whole church family into various groups and asking everyone in the church to pray for some part
- an emergency prayer 'ring-round' or email circulation, designed for responding to emergency needs, taking particular care over appropriate confidentiality
- arranging a specific time for prayer before or after services, when people who are concerned or anxious can share their burden
- encouraging the whole church to prayer, wherever they happen to be, at a set time each week.

Where people are busy, they may tend to opt for the informal through fear of yet more organizing to do, but it is helpful to remember that it is sometimes possible for housebound or otherwise physically inactive people to organize and lead such ministry. The danger of informality in this matter can be that nothing is done. Many people find that in busy lives they sometimes overlook people or things, so some planning for our praying may be the best way to keep a check on ourselves and to ensure that everyone is supported regularly.

PRAYER

It is one thing to pray *for* people and quite another to pray *with* people. Many of us might speak with some diffidence about our ability to pray for people, but this is as nothing compared to most people's reticence to pray with people. Prayer with people raises all manner of issues. When to pray? What to pray for? Such questions might seem important, but the really pressing question for most of us is to do with our sense of personal worthiness for this ministry.

There are several basic principles which can help us to pray with people.

1. None of us is offering pastoral care because we are worthy. We have our part in this ministry because others in church have seen spiritual gifts in us, and encouraged us to take up a role where we can use those gifts. If we were to decline to use them because we felt ourselves unworthy that would not be doing best either by God or by our fellow church members.

2. Our own sense of unworthiness is itself a reminder of how in all things we are dependent upon God, not just for what we do, but how we do it, day-by-day. If we seek to offer pastoral care because we feel we can do it, we shall certainly fail, but if we think it possible that God might work through us, all is possible. We call this grace.

3. How confident and comfortable, or not, we feel we are at praying is not really the point. What matters is how willing we are to try, and being willing to try is what opens the gateway to heaven. However eloquent our prayers might be, the strength of our prayers does not lie in either the quantity or energy of our words, but rather it is to be found in God's grace. God hears even our most incoherent ramblings and understands them. As Paul says, 'the Spirit helps us in our weakness; for we do not know how to pray as we ought, but that very Spirit intercedes with sighs too deep for words. And God, who searches the heart, knows what is the mind of the Spirit, because the Spirit intercedes for the saints according

to the will of God. We know that all things work together for good for those who love God, who are called according to his purpose. It comes from the enabling work of the Holy Spirit who takes our stammered words and interprets them to our Father in heaven' (Romans 8.26–28).

4 If we pray for people regularly, we are more likely to find it more comfortable praying with them.

We may have to pluck up courage the first time we come to pray with people or someone, and we may feel very vulnerable. God certainly wants us to pray with confidence and not to be afraid: 'Since, then, we have a great high priest who has passed through the heavens, Jesus, the Son of God, let us hold fast to our confession. For we do not have a high priest who is unable to sympathize with our weaknesses, but we have one who in every respect has been tested as we are, yet without sin' (Hebrews 4.14–15). If we take that passage seriously, it is clear that God wants to receive our prayers for others and that God also reassures us that we shall ourselves find whatever support we need, through God's grace. This gives us a strong foundation on which to approach the whole business of praying with people.

Here are some practical points to keep in mind:

1 The question of whether to pray with people might arise when we are their guests, either at their home or somewhere else. Everyone who is a guest should always respect the hospitality of their host, and this is just as true when we are with people in a residential care home or in a hospital. Offering pastoral care is not about proprietorial rights, but about respecting everyone's integrity.

2 If we give the impression, however inadvertent, that prayer is only for serious situations this is most unfortunate. It is clearly most natural to offer to pray with people in a moment of crisis, indeed not to do so risks heightening their distress. However, prayer is not a crisis help line; rather, it is an expression of an active relationship with God within which

are held not only troubles, but also joys and ordinariness. We could do worse than to take on board the words of the Psalmist: 'It is good to give thanks to the LORD' (Psalm 92.1). It is wise to remember that as we share times of gladness, these should be shared with God in prayers just as much as difficulties and crises.

3 Being aware of keeping an appropriate balance immediately raises the obvious question: When should we pray with people? Sometimes people will make it very clear that they would like us to pray with them, and sometimes that they would not, but often they give no clear indication of what they might like. Perhaps the best way of responding in these situations is simply to ask the question: 'Would you find it helpful if I say a prayer while I am here?' Although we may find even asking the question embarrassing, most people prefer to be asked a straightforward question, and will generally give a straightforward answer. Often that answer will be a very positive affirmation, but not always. Don't be shocked by a negative response. Once, in a hospital visit, the patient replied 'Good grief, I'm not that ill!' Whatever our opinion of the answer, it should always be respected, and no attempt made to change the person's mind. Pastoral care is about respecting integrity. In these situations, prayers need to be silent, or offered later.

4 Even when we have listened carefully to what people have said to us, it may still be the case that we have little clear idea what they want, and that might be because they themselves are not sure. When this situation arises, it is often best to ask people what they would like us to pray for. Asking such a question is not just about informing our prayers, but of much greater importance is that it can sometimes enable people to help sort out the issues in their own mind, and therefore what other areas of support they might find helpful. Even more importantly, it can prevent us leaving them with a sense of disappointment at the end of our conversation.

5 A rather different problem that we might encounter is that sometimes people may be quite clear exactly how they would like their prayers answered, but we find ourselves thinking that God may have some difficulties in granting their requests. When this occurs, we have no place to presume how God might respond, and no need to offer our opinions. Any judgementalism, however justified we may feel, is counter-productive and runs the risk of trying to do God's work ourselves. In these moments, we would be wise to keep a careful check on ourselves, so that 'our' prayer is not heard by someone as a reprimand which would, of course, separate us from them. If we were to show our opinion, we would slip into preaching instead of praying.

6 There is a lot to be said for being prepared with how we might pray with someone before we meet them. Most people do not have overly huge expectations: most people know that we do not all have A-Levels in praying, and a simple but heartfelt prayer is generally deeply appreciated. There is no reason why we could not prepare a simple generic form of prayer, and keep that in our heads or written down, with whatever personal touch seems appropriate.

7 As a word of caution, if we find ourselves reaching the point where we offer the same stale prayers regularly, or we sense our prayers are simply 'the done thing', this is a moment to be pleased with our own spiritual growth, which we do not want to frustrate. This is another moment to step out in faith. Perhaps it is a nudge from God to step away from our regular prayer that we memorized or wrote down.

Even when we have prepared a short and simple prayer, written down or learned, we might very well still find it far from easy to pray with people. It can be difficult to find out or work out their wishes, or when to ask. Sometimes we may find that even when we feel that this is a good and appropriate time to pray, we are still at a loss. Perhaps we are confused, or lacking courage at that moment. If we should not feel equal to the task of praying with people, there are two things we can do, and both of them can be surprisingly helpful:

1. We can invite people to join us in church, or we can invite them to pray about it at the same time as a group in church will be praying. By doing this we link them in with a wider group even though they might not physically be present. If we say we will do this, we must remember to do so.

2. We can identify with people by openly admitting our own difficulty in praying. If we admit our common humanity it is another important way to get alongside people. However, it could be disappointing and/or isolating to leave matters there, so we could offer to bring along someone else from church, someone we trust, to help them to pray.

Despite any anxiety we might have about praying with people, while we are meeting people, many of us find that the question in our minds is simply, 'what shall I say?' This was a question that Jesus knew that his disciples would face, and he gave specific instructions to them about this when he sent them out: 'As you enter the house, greet it' (Matthew 10.12), and he followed this with an assurance that they need not fear being lost for words: 'When they hand you over, do not worry about how you are to speak or what you are to say; for what you are to say will be given to you at that time; for it is not you who speak, but the Spirit of your Father speaking through you' (Matthew 10.19–20). Jesus gives us the same assurance, that the Holy Spirit will guide our conversations.

Instead of thinking on the way home what we could have said, if we offer a simple 'arrow prayer' while we listen to someone speaking – 'Lord, give me the words needed for this moment' – we are rather more likely to find that thoughts and ideas that surprise us are given at that moment, and perhaps later we might hear the encouragement that 'you really don't know how helpful your words were'. We might be amazed by this, but we should also be encouraged to try with more confidence another time.

When offering pastoral care, there is never any fixed form of prayer that must or should be used on any or all occasions. Some of us may feel very comfortable leading a spontaneous and unwritten prayer, known as extempore prayer, while others of us will feel more comfortable if we write a prayer in advance. Writing down a prayer in advance can help us to clarify our thoughts, control our length and time, and give us some courage when the moment comes to pray. As we share in this ministry it is an important part in the total worship of God's people.

Having said all of this, there will be some situations when the most appropriate, and deeply profound, prayer that we can offer is the Lord's Prayer. Sometimes this is all that is needed, and it is a prayer which the most surprising people might join in with in the most surprising situations, and which speaks to so many people on so many levels.

When we are using other prayers, we need not rely on our own imagination to prepare a prayer. There is a massive treasury of prayers written by many other Christians, some recently and some hundreds of years ago, some local to us, and some from around the globe. In any event, neither eloquence nor complexity are requirements of effective prayer. All God asks of us, all that the Bible teaches us, is to express the thoughts of our heart simply and directly.

Some questions for personal reflection, or discussion with others

- What do you find most challenging about prayer generally?
- How do you feel about praying for someone?
- How do you feel about praying with someone?

PRAYER

A prayer to use

Loving God, we do not understand your ways, but we believe that your love responds, and mends people who are broken in body, mind or spirit. Show us how to pray, so that through our prayers you can bring peace beyond pain, and make whole people who are broken; through Jesus Christ our Lord. Amen.

7

What is a 'visit'?

In former generations, from Georgian times until the latter years of the twentieth century, 'visiting' was a formal part of English culture. In her novel *Cranford* Elizabeth Gaskell writes of how well-to-do and aspiring people would all visit each other at set times of day. It was in that context that what many think of today as 'pastoral visiting' evolved. In the 1950s, clergy cycled around their parishes and congregations, making what might be sometimes quite formal visits to people. In some homes the best china and the family silver would come out, and cakes would be baked. Although this was a part of the social norms and cultures of the time, it didn't always facilitate helpful pastoral encounters. Furthermore, while this was very much part of upper and middle class social and ecclesiastical interaction, it wasn't the case in different situations. A nonconformist minister in 1930s Lancashire reported visiting people while they were working hard in various domestic situations; one lady who was making bread when the minister called in commented that she always baked after black leading the range to get the black lead off her fingers.

Some of the stereotypes of visiting, well within the lifetime of older church members in the 2020s, do not serve us well for patterns of pastoral care in the current age. It is, of course, true that many people will still like to be visited in their home, particularly those who are housebound and those in residential care, and those who are in hospital will often appreciate a visit. However, changes in society mean that many people are simply not used to or comfortable with being visited in their home for a variety of reasons. A greater awareness of safeguarding means that it is not always possible or appropriate to visit some vulnerable people on our own in their home. Many churches today have become much of a community hub, and a quiet conversation on comfortable chairs over a cup of coffee in a thriving church is just as much a 'visit' as calling in on someone at home. Many people will meet their friends in one of the multitude of coffee shops or pubs, and these can equally be very good places to meet people for pastoral care. In the digital age, where young people live almost entirely online, some will look for pastoral care online, through messaging and email. A global pandemic reminded many of the value of a telephone call. A greater range of options to offer pastoral care to people, once we have turned our minds in this direction, is far from a barrier to pastoral care but in fact a means by which more pastoral care can be offered to more people more easily, but also requires more care. In their statements on ministry, most denominations do not mention pastoral visiting, and instead tend to speak of pastoral care, leadership and oversight. This is significant, and reminds us that what we are about is pastoral care, which is wider than just 'visiting'. In this context, I prefer to think of a pastoral 'encounter' rather than a 'visit'. An 'encounter' might well take place in someone's home or a hospital, but it might also take place in a café or on church premises. It might be online, and it might be a shared train journey in commuter areas. The possibilities are very broad once we think creatively about pastoral 'encounters'.

Just as there are a variety of pastoral 'encounters', it is equally important to realize that there are many different patterns of pastoral care across many different churches. What works well in one place will not work so well in another. No two churches have identical circumstances. There is ample opportunity for those giving pastoral care to respond to their own situation in the best way possible to ensure that everyone within the family of their church is properly cared for. Pastoral care must be seen in this context if future problems are to be avoided.

Spending time with people offering pastoral care is not a neutral activity. What I mean by this is that in disturbed and troubled times, people will probably be anxious to know whether we come in peace and friendship. Those who are in any way anxious about their relationship with the church will often have questions like these in their minds. Some people will not automatically assume that our offer of pastoral care is on their side. Very occasionally, contact with someone may have to do with a matter of church discipline or to resolve some form of dispute, but our call in the ordinary run of pastoral care is trying to be something of God with people and for people.

Pastoral care in a Christian context, as opposed to friendship in a secular social context, has to do with imparting blessing. In Luke 9 Jesus sent his disciples out to bless people. The disciples were given authority and instruction so that the people of the towns and villages they came to might know that the power of God had visited them. They were to act so that the presence of God would be made plain. Paul had a similar motivation in mind when he wrote about his plans to visit the church in Corinth (2 Corinthians). Paul was trying to work together with the Corinthians for their own happiness. This working together-with is the activity which tells them how much Paul loves them all.

In Matthew's Gospel Jesus issues a stark challenge over the importance of pastoral care: 'I was hungry and you gave me food, I was thirsty and you gave me something to drink, I was a stranger and you welcomed me, I was naked and you gave me clothing, I was sick and you took care of me, I was in prison and you visited me' (Matthew 25.35–36). This passage is all about the provision for the whole person:

- food and drink (nourishment)
- hospitality (acceptance)
- clothing for the naked (personal dignity)
- care for the sick (compassion)
- visiting (community).

Pastoral encounters may be either planned or spontaneous, and planned encounters may be either formal or informal. We shall need all three types of encounter at one time or another.

WHAT IS A 'VISIT'?

Planning

Though churches vary enormously, every church has some form of list of the people who are associated with it, whether formal membership or linked through some form of looser affiliation. Every church, whether large or small, is therefore able to plan to some extent its approach to pastoral care. In most churches there is an intention to see that some pastoral care is offered, even if this is delegated to a small number. Whether working on a large scale with a multiplicity of cell groups, or in a small church where formal groups are clearly inappropriate, it is possible to plan the pastoral care of those in the church's care. The object must be to ensure that everyone within the community of the church experiences the love and care of the church.

This objective will only be secured if it is planned. If we don't plan the pastoral care of our congregations it is not likely to happen. The logic of planning the overall pastoral care of the congregation is that where people specifically involved are each given a list of people to look after they must plan the care within their list. The actual plan adopted will certainly vary very considerably from place to place and from person to person, but it will probably need to allow for both formal and informal encounters.

Formal encounters

The formal encounter is likely to be one in which we have been asked to find out certain information from the members we are responsible for, or we are responding to a known pastoral situation such as a birth in the family, an accident, or an illness. In this context formal means planned and arranged in advance, rather than the style of the encounter. In such circumstances it is almost always most appropriate to make contact in advance to arrange a convenient time to meet, even if that is in five minutes' time. Arranging to meet people in advance will sometimes be essential if we are able to make sensible use of whatever time we have available.

Informal encounters

The informal encounter is likely to be that made when dropping in with a small gift, popping in to call to offer birthday wishes, an 'over-the-garden-wall' conversation which results in an invitation to come in for a cup of coffee, and so on. In some communities informal encounters may happen all the time around a village or town. Some Welsh communities speak of this as 'taking considerably longer to walk down the village street than planned'. However, frequent informal contact must not allow those we happen not to have seen this way to be neglected, nor for us to lose sight of others in our care. It is unlikely that we shall develop pastoral care in any depth if we encounter only when there is some item of church business or personal concern to be dealt with. There is very good reason to include some socializing in our encountering. Encountering people without strings can sometimes do more to deepen personal relationships than any number of formal encounters which inevitably carry concealed pressure points.

If we are going to keep a balance in our encounters with people, we may find some form of record keeping is helpful. However, we need to be very careful indeed not to note down any personal information about people, and to keep all our notes confidential.

If we are praying regularly for people, and we are encountering them one way or another, we may find from time to time that a name will come into mind for no apparent reason. This may happen when we are actually on the way to an encounter with someone else, in which case we shouldn't be surprised if our planned encounter proves to be shorter than we had allowed for, or if our informal encounter finds no one at home. What may be happening is that God is guiding our pastoral care. We need to respond to promptings like this when they come into

WHAT IS A 'VISIT'?

our mind. Call in to see that person. Time and again when I have followed up such promptings, I have been greeted with words such as 'I'm so glad to see you', 'I was going to contact you because …', 'Thank goodness …'. Even if we don't get that response at that moment, there's no need to be disappointed. God may still be preparing the ground for what is yet to be. As people of faith, we work in faith, and so our responses need to be offered in faith. We need to thank God for prompting us, and then commit that encounter to God's providential use for the long-term blessing of that person.

To end this chapter, here are ten rules for pastoral encounters:

1 We must always remember that we are visitors, and when calling on someone at their home never forget the four cardinal words 'May I come in?' These words are a courteous beginning to a conversation and the courtesy will normally be taken positively, unless it is an inconvenient time, or the person is unwell. To more frail people who can't get to the door themselves, they are words that preserve some personal dignity and the offering of the gift of hospitality. Even where you have been given access to a key to let yourself in to someone unable to answer their door, it is always important to check if it is convenient and appropriate to come in.

2 We must not outstay our welcome. We must watch our host's body language and be aware of the time – either or both will tell us when it is time to go, but we do need to stay long enough to have a meaningful conversation with them. However, do not look at your own watch if you can possibly avoid it – that gives an immediate signal that we are in a hurry, even if we are not. If there is a clock in the room, or if our host's watch is in a line of sight, these can be helpful ways to keep an eye on the time sensitively.

3 We must be prepared to receive. Any healthy relationship is a two-way process. As a guest we have gifts to offer to those we encounter. We shouldn't be reluctant to accept 'gifts' in

return. In particular, when visiting elderly or frail people, it can be helpful to accept the offer of a cup of tea, and to let them actually make it – even if it is painful to watch them struggling to do so. Obviously, it is not appropriate to accept money, or significant or valuable gifts. Gifts should certainly never be solicited.

4 If we say we'll do something, we must do it. If we find we can't do it at once for some reason, we should provide an update.

5 We must guard with our life anything told to us in confidence, unless some discloses an intention to harm themselves or someone else, to commit a criminal offence, or discloses abuse. If someone is seeking help, or looking for some other involvement, we should ask their permission to tell someone else, such as the minister.

6 We must not encourage gossip or closet criticism. If someone raises a cause for concern, particularly a criticism of some thing or someone, it is unhelpful to offer to pass it on, to take it up anonymously on their behalf, or to join in gossip. It is far better to help someone work out their thinking, and present their own case, even if we don't agree with it ourselves.

7 We should avoid firing other people's bullets. We must never, just never, use someone else's concern or complaint as an excuse for firing off any matters of our own. We must have the courage to accept full responsibility for what we want to say. Mention others only with their permission. People will not trust us if they feel we will misuse what they say to us.

8 It is wrong to apologize for taking up someone's time. Their time and ours alike are given by God. If we need to apologize for wasting their time, we are wasting our time.

WHAT IS A 'VISIT'?

9 A phone call, email, card posted, text message etc. can be very valuable, and show people that they are not forgotten. However, none of those can ever be a perpetual replacement for a personal encounter when people are wanting that.

10 As well as going to meet people, whether in their home or elsewhere, we might also invite them to meet us or come to our home. Our personal circumstances may not always permit it, and we shouldn't feel badly about it if they don't, but where they do the invitation to visit us can be a sign to them that a genuine relationship is being sought.

Some questions for personal reflection, or discussion with others

- How do you respond to ideas that there are many other ways to offer people pastoral care beyond visiting them in their home?
- Where do you feel the balance lies between spontaneity and informality versus planning?
- Do the ten rules need adding to, reducing, changing, or do they cover everything?

A prayer to use

God, in Jesus we saw how you always searched out the lost. Help us to find your people wherever they may be, and in your love give us the creativity to care for each and all, whatever the cost may be. We pray in Jesus' name. Amen.

8

Caring for families and children

Please don't skip this chapter because you have no children in church on a Sunday morning! This may seem irrelevant to many churches because many churches do not have children and families as a part of their Sunday congregation; however, even where churches are in that position, there may still be children and families involved in Messy Church, children's activity groups, toddler groups or uniformed organizations, and where there is a strong relationship it would be unwise to discount groups meeting on the premises.

Someone in a church once said that they found it difficult going to see Alex and Sam because the children never seemed to go to bed, and were never anywhere but around their parents, and it was hard to have a conversation without the children. By contrast someone else said that when they visited Robin and Chris they felt they had no way of getting to know their children at all. A third person lamented that they hadn't had any children in their church for a very long time.

Many people feel confused when considering the place of children and families in the life of the church. Those of a certain age are all too aware of how churches were once packed with children and families, or so they recall. Hindsight can sometimes be rose-tinted. This confusion becomes even more acute when we consider pastoral care of children and families. The vast majority of us instinctively relate far more readily to adults than to children, although a few are clearly gifted to relate easily to children. The wider issue is really how we, as a congregation, look after children.

In doing so we have responsibilities that are both moral and legal. Legal responsibilities began under the Children Act 1989, which started a process of legally enshrining good practice in the care of children. Several pieces of legislation have followed, and this underpins church safeguarding, which is *de facto* a legal responsibility, particularly in the light of the Independent Inquiry into Child Sexual Abuse of the late 2010s and early 2020s. Any legislation which comes from IICSA will add to legal underpinning of what is our moral responsibility to keep children and other vulnerable people safe.

Each church, through whatever body bears legal and trustee responsibilities in the church, has a responsibility for the children of the church, and to be sure that care for them is not only given but given safely. The exact way in which this will work out in practice will vary from church to church according to circumstances. In churches which have organized children's activities on a Sunday or during the week, the responsibility is to ensure that the leaders are given every help and encouragement, and to ensure that the care given to the children is the very best.

These responsibilities extend beyond safeguarding: children's work needs some of the church's budget to be done well and safely, even if the church has to find a bit more money. It also means encouraging leaders to attend appropriate training from time to time. It also means preparations for baptisms, part of which includes making the service accessible and welcoming to people not used to church. It may mean reminding those who see the children as 'the church of tomorrow' that they are properly part of the church of today, with their faith which will undoubtedly be as acceptable to God as the faith of any adults.

It means ensuring that the patterns of worship of the church are such that children have proper access to the full diet of worship. In some churches it may mean working harder at finding leaders. Too often the task of securing any assistance in the Junior Church or other youth organizations is left to the leaders themselves, even to the extent of finding their own successors when for good reason they have to give up the work they have been doing. It is all too common to hear good people, including leaders of children's and youth activities, saying that they feel guilty at giving up. Many of us know leaders who didn't give up when they should have done. It cannot be in the best interests of our children for them to be cared for by people whose heart is not in it or who are riddled with guilt at even the thought of retiring. Equally it is part of the church's responsibility to have the courage to 'release' leaders who really should no longer be leading. To let matters drift on because we are afraid of hurting or upsetting people is to deny our children the proper care we must provide for them. How we deal with these situations sets the culture and ethos of the church's care of its children.

It is all too easy to be relieved to have found people willing to lead children's work, but each church also has a responsibility for the quality of that work, not just that it exists. Children's work is not just child care or entertainment, but a part of their growth in their Christian faith. Are we doing all that we can to encourage that? What kind of pastoral care do we exercise towards children? Are they visited when ill? Are their birthdays remembered? Does anyone bother to find out why they haven't been for the past three weeks? Other questions will, of course, be equally important.

If this passage has made you feel uncomfortable, perhaps something is wrong in our church if the only time we pay attention to children is when there is a problem. If, however, we have relationships in the church that are characterized by ongoing encouragement and support, the atmosphere will surely be right.

The number of children within a congregation is sometimes used as a measure of the health of a local church. It is not unusual for people to feel that a church has no future without children. When the mood is like that, the absence of children has become a problem, sapping both the energy of the congregation and the ability of the leaders to offer an effective ministry to the people who are there. The absence of children then becomes a dispiriting element in the life of the church. There are several things that can be done about this.

CARING FOR FAMILIES AND CHILDREN

1 **Challenge the assumption:** Is it really true that a church without children has no future? The answer may well depend on the kind of community in which the church is situated. In an area overwhelmingly populated by retired people, there may indeed be few children but that does not have to prevent the church being a growing church. There may be more than enough retired people both to regenerate the congregation and also to enable it to grow. Even if the community itself is declining, and there are indeed no children about, each and every church is challenged to respond to and care for the community that does exist. This responsibility must not be side-stepped simply because once there were children and now there are none.

2 **Ask the question:** 'Is it inevitable that this church has no children within it?' In order to answer this churches must search out the facts. Are there children in the local community? If there are, are they attending other local churches? All too often churches will say that theirs is a retirement area without children when a cursory glance at the supermarkets and the schools will make it clear that this is nonsense. If there are children in the community then the challenge becomes how to make contact with the children who are there. However many there are, it is likely that only a very few will have any form of contact with any church. Churches need to consider: Why do these children not come to our church? What stops them? What do they want us to offer them? When do we need to offer things to fit into the pattern of family life today? Does our image inadvertently exclude people, rather than welcome them? Are our ideas too narrow? Are there specific needs that we could try to meet? Only when we have faced squarely questions such as these will we be able to take any steps.

3 **Do the research:** How can we find out why our church doesn't have any children? Some of the information we need will be of a general kind, but some will be specific to

our own church. Generally speaking, people working in the community with children, such as school teachers and governors, youth groups, uniformed organizations, or existing children's group leaders, may well be happy to share their understanding of the community in general terms.

4 **Harness the goodwill:** Even today, despite much perceived indifference to churches, there remains a significant level of goodwill towards local churches which exists in many communities. This is a valuable resource, and we leave it untapped at our peril. Even in the 2020s, many churches think of themselves as a provider for the community, but the reality is that churches are also receivers of what the community can do for them. For generations, many churches have sought to give out the good news, but not really considered what they can receive from their community. One of the important things the community does have is contact with many people that churches simply do not. Communities reach the people that church cannot. One way forward for the church without children to explore is to harness the goodwill of the community as a first step. Many people share the church's concern for the children in our communities. There is nothing to be lost and everything to be gained from inviting some of those who share this concern to explore with us what can be done. If we can manage to do this it needs to be without the presumption that it can only be done properly if the church does it or has total control over how it is done. Any initiative of this sort will need a serious commitment of time and energy to carry it through.

5 **Use imagination:** Being church needs a lot of imagination generally. We need to dream dreams and then to let the creative sparks fly as we share together in how to make them a reality. Too often, we either lack or are afraid to use imagination. Too often, we are afraid to create precedents. Too often, problems that we have encountered in the past are more dominant than the vision we have of the future.

CARING FOR FAMILIES AND CHILDREN

Too often our answers to recurring problems are doing the same thing as before. Yet as Christians it is our privilege to trust the promise of God, 'See, I am making all things new' (Revelation 21.5). Nowhere should this be more evident than in the way we take seriously our responsibility for the children in our church and community.

How we think about all of these issues, and the attitude with which we look for solutions, will have a profound effect upon the shape of what we are able to do. Do we assume that we have to meet the needs from within the church community? Those in small churches who have read this far may have already concluded that these ideas are only for larger churches and that they are beyond their own small congregation. Those in the larger churches will know that such problems are not limited to smaller churches. Pretty much all churches have recruitment problems, not least because there are more jobs to be done more carefully by fewer and older people. Can the answers to these questions be found in the goodwill towards our church in the surrounding community?

Even in the 2020s, there remains significant goodwill towards local churches in most communities, even if there is indifference to the wider church, but how much real goodwill is there in the local church towards the community it is part of? Are we praying that the local school will find the governors it needs? Are we supporting the Guides and Scouts with our prayers? Do we ever respond to the public invitations to come along to the mother and toddler group tabletop sale? Do we go along when the local school has its summer fair? Are we prepared to campaign for the council to provide an area where young people can skateboard in safety and with a minimum of nuisance to others? The list is endless once we begin to develop an awareness of, and interest in, our community.

It is both a good biblical principle, and a sensible way of life, to treat others as we wish to be treated ourselves. If we want people to come to church when we advertise events, we should be alert to events going on in the community and support them.

If we support only the children and youth activities of our own church, we are guilty of self-interest. Clearly, we can't do all these things by ourselves. What we can do is to ensure that such matters are included in the conversation when our church talks about work among the young. We can try to ensure that encouragement is given to the church community to be broad in its interests and warm-hearted in its response.

In such ways we can show that our care for the children and young people of the church is both as full and as genuine as it should be. We shall fail to do this if we are only interested in what is being promoted by our own or other churches. Separating the sacred and secular too firmly is not helpful in building networks and relationships in and with the community, and likewise it would be a doubtless unintended spiritual arrogance if we ever belittled those who provide for children and young people in other organizations.

This chapter began with the simple question of how we offer pastoral care to children and families. By now we know that the answer requires rather more work and thought on the part of the church than we might have first imagined. There is no doubt that the problems outlined at the start of this chapter are real ones. Most of us do find it much easier to relate to adults than to children. There are a number of reasons for this.

1 **The problem of access:** How can we engage with children without them feeling inhibited by their parents? The honest answer has to be only with the utmost difficulty, and it would be unwise to try.

2 **The problem of relationship:** What relationship are we seeking with the children? Children's friendships ebb and flow, and are shaped by peer group pressures, passing interests and shared activities. In many instances, these seem increasingly to separate the children from the adults as adolescence approaches.

3 **The problem of definition:** What do we mean by the pastoral care of children? We have explored the corporate responsi-

bility of the church towards children, but how does this relate to each individual child?

Working properly within an appropriate culture of safeguarding, there is very limited scope for us to develop pastoral care for children in the way that we do for adults. There are at least two positive elements that we can identify as appropriate in our care of children.

1 **Inclusive activities.** One way that we can better care for families with children is to be much more intentional about activities for all age groups, and that does not mean simply expecting children to do what the adults want! All too often our meetings are mainly for adults, and very often they are arranged in the evening and for purposes which are ill-suited to the inclusion of children. However, in the different setting of a group family barbecue or picnic, children can feel included from the beginning, even more so if there are games for all ages to play together. The fact that adults can have fun as part of their life in the church is surely an important lesson for children to learn. Churches need not be dull and boring, and there are many benefits to the whole church from learning this. It is crucial to discuss with parents what times work for them. Careful account needs to be taken not just of bed times, but meal times, routines, other activities, and traffic at rush hour. However we do it, the important thing is that children are included in ways that don't separate. Many churches are familiar with learning to include women and men, and all ethnicities, and are beginning to learn how to include all genders. It is just as important that we develop the life of the church as a community of people of all ages. Not everyone is comfortable with children, and it is fine for some things to be designed for adults only, so long as there is plenty of appropriate provision for children. Inclusive activities need to inspire both children and adults, and trying to do that is just as much part of the pastoral care we are trying to offer.

2. **Creative prayer.** In the chapter on prayer I tried to make clear that prayer is the most practical activity within our pastoral care, and this needs to be emphasized again in our pastoral care of children. There is no greater gift we can impart to children than our prayers. There is nothing more likely both to support and build an ongoing relationship with them than our prayers for them. There is surely nothing better that we can do than to pray God's blessing for them. God has a purpose for each of them. Each one needs help in discovering that purpose and owning it for themselves, just as all adults do. The way has to be prepared if that is to happen. Before children can do this for themselves, windows of opportunity need to be opened for God to work. This is, in part, the task of Christian parenthood; and in part, the task of the Christian community as it cares for the young. Our role as those offering pastoral care can be crucial if that part is to be effective. One minister told the story of how during his teenage years, when churchgoing had fallen out of fashion, two people in the church in which he grew up never stopped praying for him. From time to time they found ways of reminding him of what they were doing. It annoyed him a great deal at the time, but some years later he was called to the ministry. Looking back, he said that he was convinced that the prayers of those two people during his difficult adolescent years were a vital part of the preparation for the call to ministry to be heard and answered. If we strive to make our pastoral care systematic, and our prayers regular and informed, these can all be used effectively to assist us in praying for children and young people. This can be taken a step further if we also positively affirm their special days – their birthdays and other days which mark the stages in growing-up, their personal achievements, and so on. If, in our prayers, we have positive attitudes towards the children and young people as individuals we shall be much better placed to offer them pastoral care.

CARING FOR FAMILIES AND CHILDREN

In 1990 the General Assembly of the United Reformed Church agreed a Charter for Children in the church. However, it is not denominational, and the points are relevant to all churches. The original wording is normal print, with a more recently agreed simplified wording in italics:

Children are equal partners with adults in the life of the church.
Children in our church are just as important as adults.

The full diet of Christian worship is for children as well as adults.
Everybody in our church can worship God in lots of different ways, no matter how old they are.

Learning is for the whole church, adults and children.
Our church helps everybody keep on learning.

Fellowship is for all – each belonging meaningfully to the rest.
Our church is a place where everyone feels and knows they belong.

Service is for children to give, as well as adults.
In our church. children can do things to help God, the church and other people.

The call to evangelism comes to all God's people of whatever age. God wants everybody to share his good news with others.
Our church listens and helps us share what we have learned.

The Holy Spirit speaks powerfully through children as well as adults.
People can learn what God wants to say to them through what we say and do. Our church listens to children too.

The discovery and development of gifts in children and adults is a key function of the church.
Our church helps us find our 'thing' and grow in it.

As a church community we must learn to do only those things in separate age groups which we cannot in all conscience do together.
Our church gives us lots of opportunities to do things with everyone else and doesn't have loads of things which are just for adults.

The concept of the 'Priesthood of all Believers' includes children.
Everyone in our church can be equally close to God; praying and serving.

Some questions for personal reflection, or discussion with others

- What do you think about planning for ways to engage children in the life of the church?

- If you visit families, do you feel more like you're visiting Alex and Sam, or Robin and Chris?

- How do you respond to the Charter for Children in the church?

A prayer to use

God of life, you have shaped us in your image, and filled us with wisdom and love, so that we and all your children may know and love you. Help us to find ways to care for children and families, so that we always respect their dignity and lead them to flourish in life, always following the example of your son, Jesus Christ our Lord. Amen.

9

Caring for sick people

For many people, our first thought about pastoral care is visiting people who are sick. It may be our first experience of pastoral care, and equally it might be our first introduction to some of the people who seek our pastoral care. Visiting people who are ill is a deeply biblical concept, mentioned many times throughout the Bible. It is also a deeply human instinct to try to care for people who are ill, whether in body or mind or spirit. If suffering was what God wanted, then when Jesus healed people he would have been working against God, and that is not possible. This is why many of us feel some kind of inner compulsion and sense of priority to visit people who are sick. This is also the moment, perhaps more than any other, when people may feel neglected if we do not visit them.

Our own response

How most of us feel about illness and suffering will have been shaped to some extent by the attitudes of our parents or of those closest to us when we were children, and it may also have been influenced by our own experiences of illness and suffering when we were very young. Naturally, our early influences will also have been supplemented by more recent encounters with illness and suffering, and these might have confirmed our childhood feelings or they might have led us now to having very different thoughts and feelings on illness and suffering. Our thoughts today may have been developed by other experiences, or by books that we have read. Some people find fulfilment in trying to offer hope to those who are ill or suffering, while others will find the whole experience troubling. It is not unusual to meet people who are distinctly uncomfortable around hospitals.

It has to be said that many of us are sometimes a little confused, and not always consistent, in our approach to illness and suffering. Many of us experience some personal confusion when we are ill. For much of life, many of us will reject illness, and fight strongly to live, while in our later years we may come to view illness as the prelude to entering eternal life, or at least as a way of escaping from mounting inner frustration, as illness and frailty increasingly limit our quality of life and make us ever more dependent on others. A whole industry of professional carers has arisen, and advances in drug treatments mean many of us live for far longer than was the case a couple of generations ago. However, I have lost count of the number of people who have told me not to get old because getting old is no fun. It is very likely that these varied feelings will be with us when we are visiting the sick and that they will affect the tone of, and perhaps even shape, our conversations.

Just as each of us has a different perspective on, and response to, illness and suffering so other people, too, will have mixed thoughts and feelings on the subject. While everyone has a different view, we are likely to encounter two main attitudes to illness and suffering. One is a rooted opposition to the very concept of illness: this opposition might be built on either the customs of our contemporary society which has invested so much energy and funding in health promotion and care, or by a strong biblical sense that sickness and suffering do not belong in the Kingdom of God, or a combination of both of these. Those who hold this view might point out that 80% of the recorded activity of Jesus is to do with healing the sick. The other attitude that we are likely to encounter is people who, with varying degrees of reluctance, accept the situation of illness and suffering. They may not deny that the massive developments in health care are right for the nation and have brought many good things to many people, but they might still ask whether each person has an inherent right to permanent good health. They may express doubts about the wisdom of some major treatments which cost massive sums of money and the strenuous efforts that often seem to be made to keep elderly people alive. Those who hold such views may point out that the Bible appears to show that God can use sickness within God's purposes of love, that Jesus did not heal everyone he came across who was sick, and that there are very many people who are severely afflicted and suffer constant pain, yet are radiant and Christ-like.

Working through the theology of illness and suffering would take a whole book of its own and more, but it is enough for us to recognize that we shall meet a wide variety of thoughts and feelings as we offer pastoral care to people who are ill and suffering. We will surely find these variations within ourselves as much as in anyone else, and it is more than likely that as we gain more experience we shall find that our own thoughts and feelings change.

What is most important is that we do not allow our feelings to result in a negative reaction to things that shock us. If we do allow that, we shall almost certainly become judgemental and the opportunity for pastoral care will pass. It is vital to remember that there is usually a reason why people say or do the things they do. For instance, we may find it deeply shocking that a man never visited his partner while they were in hospital having surgery. His explanation that he couldn't stand the smell of hospitals seems a little thin. Yet the man may have this phobia because he is remembering, perhaps subconsciously, the hospital visits that he made as a youngster when his mother or father or grandparent was dying.

In a similar way, the woman who has no time for illness, and appears to have little sympathy with anyone who is ill, especially those who are nearest and dearest, may have watched someone deeply loved enduring a painful death. Her family's illnesses reawaken the terrible power of that experience, and thereby raise doubts about her ability to cope. They speak about dying and death, and she is very frightened of both, so much so that she will be angry when members of her family are ill.

It may be easy enough to feel shocked when someone is cross because their child is ill. Set in the context of the parent's life, that anger is actually a measure of the pastoral care that is needed. It is important, therefore, to try to offer pastoral care in a way which does not limit the potential for God to meet people whatever their thoughts and feelings about illness and suffering, or whatever our personal understanding. God is bigger than any individual, and can still work where we find it difficult, but it is helpful not to make it harder for God than we need to.

In general terms, most people are expecting us to be fellow Christians who are particularly concerned for them at this point and are trying to a good neighbour. They are not expecting us to be professional carers, trained counsellors, or some form of faith healer, but they will hope that we may, in some sense, offer them some pastoral care. This pastoral care has several parts to it. These include:

- affirming their personal worth
- showing the church's concern for them
- trying to support them at a time of personal need
- using the opportunity to help them to feel 'in touch' with God
- some reassurance of support for their family
- some sympathy and understanding beyond saying words.

Knowing these points is enough for now. There is no formula which we can apply when visiting people who are ill. There is no right way to do this or say that, though there are some ways which may be more helpful than others. At its root, visiting someone who is ill springs out of the relationship between people, and will be as varied as the people involved.

It is important to remember that our visit is an aspect of the overall ministry of encouragement which we are trying to offer through pastoral care. That doesn't mean we must be optimistic in every situation: our good sense should tell us when we need to be realistic and not to get involved in creating wrong expectations. We shall, however, want to make the visit such that the person who is ill, and the ones caring day by day, will feel in some sense we have improved the situation.

It is always encouraging in pastoral care to hear people saying that they always feel better after we have visited, or that they look forward to our coming. What it is about a visit that leads to these kinds of results is impossible to define, because it is a combination of both good relationships and God working through our time together. If we pray before we visit someone in need, and have a prayerful attitude, ought we not to expect that God can somehow make it enriching no matter how ill the person is? It is also important to remember that we are not expected to have answers for every question, or to be able to solve every problem. Our role is simply to be a good neighbour, not to be able to explain everything ourselves.

End of life care is very different now from a generation or two ago. Many people who might once have received medical treatment in a hospital or hospice are able to receive appropriate end of life care at home. We are far more likely to find ourselves visiting someone in a 'hospital bed' with medical care at home than we once were. In some of these situations, I have found that it is not unusual for people to wish to say prayers they learned many years ago, sometimes as children; even if it might not be the most theologically apt prayer ever, such prayers are heartfelt and represent a depth of faith which can touch even the hardest heart,

Many ministers will have taken Holy Communion to people in their home or hospital, if they are not well enough to get to church. In doing so, we have made use of a variety of orders of service and liturgies from various denominations. Some churches authorize lay people to take bread and wine from a church service, or to preside at a celebration of Holy Communion in such situations. (The rules of the denomination about the reserved sacrament or about the authorization of lay people to preside must always be respected in both the spirit and the letter.) Such services are often very simple, and when we are able to use a form of service which is familiar to people it can be a great comfort. I once visited a lady who had spent much of her life in the Church of England, and she asked me to use the Book of Common Prayer liturgy. Even though this is completely outside the liturgical experience of the United Reformed Church, and it was clear this was not a Church of England service, those words meant a great deal to the person hearing them, so much so that she joined in almost every word that I said from memory. Many people find that as they get older, and closer to the end of their life, simple words and ideas are the ones which are best able to express their thoughts and feelings. The more that we are able to discover what those are for any particular person (it will not be the Book of Common Prayer for everyone) and reflect them in our ministry at the bedside, the greater will be the blessing bestowed on them.

When we are offering pastoral care to people who are ill or suffering we enter into a very personal relationship with the ill person, but this is not just personal because our pastoral care is an expression of the care we seek to give on behalf of the whole local church. This begs some questions of how each church responds to concern for those who are ill. While it is true that some people prefer not to be the focus of attention, it is also true that this is precisely the moment when the reality of Christian fellowship can be most under scrutiny and found to be lacking if nothing is done. It is sadly not unusual for no one to let the church know when someone is ill, and the message that someone is now home again after five days in hospital is very frustrating. However, when the message comes that someone is ill, and no one makes any contact or visits, then the church may find itself accused of indifference, and if this is the norm it will not be long before the church gains a reputation for not caring. This is a reminder, then, that we need to have a certain level of organization and system to our pastoral care, appropriate to the size and complexity of our church, while at the same time also remembering the personal responsibility of each member to be a caring person. It is always wise to keep this balance under review.

As we get to know the people to whom we are asked to offer pastoral care we shall find that they have different gifts. If we are especially aware of people who have a strong interest in people and a lively faith, these are people that we could ask to support us with their prayers. Many people have affirmed that it is the knowledge of the prayers of others that makes their work possible, especially in their more difficult times. Surely we will offer better pastoral care if we are aware of the encouragement that comes from the prayers of others.

We might also share the responsibility for the care of those who are ill with other people in the church. Most of us will want to keep pastoral encounters with people ourselves but there is good reason for us not to share it with others. Encouraging other people to share in pastoral care is also a way that we encourage them to grow and develop if they share the work of pastoral care with us.

The church's ministry to people who are ill, and our own part in that, begins long before anyone is ill or suffering. It begins as the appropriate people in the local church plan together to ensure that our pastoral care is effective. This will mean that we need to address questions such as:

- How can we make it easy for people to let the church know if anyone is ill?
- How can we help people to let their family know that they would like someone from church to know if they are ill?
- Does that awareness extend throughout the congregation, or is it limited to those who are prominent in the church?
- Is our pastoral care coordinated so that three people don't call on the same afternoon, and no one else calls all week?
- Is our pastoral care sustained throughout a person's illness, or is it enthusiastic at the beginning and patchy as time goes on?
- Is the focus of our attention just on the person who is ill, or does it include the needs of the whole family?
- Is our pastoral care limited to spiritual matters, or does it include routine practical needs?
- Conversely, if our emphasis is on practical needs, how might we better meet people's spiritual needs?

- Do our worship, preaching, Bible study and indeed the general ethos that these shape in our church, encourage church members to care for one another, or have we delegated care to specific people?
- How do we engage the whole church in praying when people have particular needs?
- Should we have a special time of prayer for people with particular needs, perhaps as a midweek service or prayer meeting?
- Do we know how we might respond if any of our members should ask for the laying on of hands or for anointing?
- Do we have an effective system of offering Holy Communion to people who are unable to get to church, and which meets all our denominational rules?
- Where appropriate, do we have a system for the distribution of flowers after services which is an expression of the church's support to people in particular need?

What we do individually, as people offering pastoral care, always needs to be seen in the context of the whole church's care for people who are in particular need. This means that everyone benefits from the framework of a considered policy agreed and understood by the church, and the active support of everyone able and willing.

All these things to consider might leave us thinking the work of pastoral care is ours, but our pastoral care is always and wholly the work of God; we are merely God's agents who express God's grace. We need therefore to offer pastoral care with as much graciousness as we can, because that is what God is. This means that we should seek to observe all the usual courtesies of life as best we can.

People who are ill or suffering often feel that they have lost control over their own lives, and that they are now in the hands of others. It is important, therefore, to allow them as much dignity and the chance to have some influence over things as we are able. By using words such as 'may I ...?' and 'I wonder if ...?' we can avoid presumption, and we can affirm a person's worth just at a time when complete dependence on others may be causing as much anxiety or distress as the illness itself.

Affirming someone's worth is important at every stage of life, and it remains so even when people appear to be seriously ill. It is always inappropriate to talk about people within their hearing, rather than to them ('Does he take sugar?'). Many families have sat at the bedside of their loved one who is in a very deep coma, and not expected to live more than a few hours. No one should be like the family that talked through how they would divide their loved one's possessions between them, only to find a few days later their loved one came out of the coma with precise knowledge of the items to which each member of the family had laid claim. Once they were out and about again one of their earliest calls was to their solicitor to make a new will. However unintended, such a conversation gives the clear impression that someone's possessions are more important to their family than they themselves are, and that their greed prevents them giving the support needed at a critical time in their loved one's life. Few of us think that could happen to us, and we may be shocked to think it would, yet these things do happen. Our pastoral care should not diminish anyone as a person. It is of the utmost importance that we affirm the positive things of life even when people appear to be close to death.

Laying on of hands and anointing with oil

We should also try to be positive when our offer of pastoral care to people who are ill produces something that we have not expected. At that point most of us find it all too easy to be anything but positive and even to appear less than gracious. Two possibilities that might be very unusual to many of us are, first, requests to lay on hands and, second, to anoint with oil, although reading chapter 5 of the letter of James shows us that these are not new.

It is very likely that many of us will never have been asked to do either of these, and we might never be asked. In fact, the whole thing may be a complete mystery to us. We might have heard the terms laying on hands or anointing, but have no mental image to give us a picture of it, or we may have an impression that it is something more to do with cults than with our kind of church.

In some churches healing services are held from time to time. In other churches such matters, sometimes called offering 'ministry', have developed into patterns of prayers and laying on of hands. Someone asking for laying on of hands or anointing may have been influenced by this, and may feel that it is a very proper part of a Christian response to illness and an expression of a deep personal commitment to God. We also need to be aware that such requests may have sprung from an entirely different motivation. If someone is feeling utterly desperate in the face of their illness, it is possible that such a request is made because they feel that all else has failed, and in that situation it may have little to do with commitment but rather more reveal the emotions of someone who feels hurt and increasingly let down by God.

How should we react if we are asked either to arrange laying on of hands or anointing? Our first reaction might be one of shock if the request goes beyond our experience. Indeed, it may awaken fears in us that it relates to an area of Christian experience which is outside the experience and the comfort of many, or it may produce anxiety about doing anything that creates false expectations for the person who is ill.

The passage in the letter of James is very clear that a number of things are involved: the initiative lies with the person who is ill to request this, and a group of leaders are to exercise this ministry. Healing is not necessarily about curing, but rather about finding a way to wholeness, which sometimes might be in other ways than curing, and it relates to the total person, so must deal with the inner realities as well as the physical symptoms. Even if we read the letter of James, and find that what is described is not hard to grasp as a concept, we may still find it very difficult to handle when requests for this ministry arrive unexpectedly. Indeed, we may find it very challenging personally.

We may feel that whoever this passage is speaking about it cannot be about us. Many of us probably think that our faith is not the kind of faith that heals sick people, nor that we possess the sort of goodness that can have such a powerful effect. If that is so, our response to the request for laying on of hands or anointing might well include having to deal with our own bewilderment, which might be almost as challenging to us as the illness is to the person who is ill. The person making the request will almost certainly be quite unaware of the bewilderment that their request has created for us. They would be most unlikely to have made that request if they thought it would trouble us. We may want to respond positively, even if this is hitherto unknown in our church and we have little knowledge of how to deal with the situation. Another possibility is that we may feel very negative towards the request while at the same time recognizing that to say 'no' would cause deep disappointment, indeed probably inflict a lot of hurt. Whatever we feel ourselves about these issues, this is neither the time to start a theological debate about the interpretation of James 5, nor the time to raise false expectations.

Unless we belong to a church that already has experience of laying on of hands and anointing and has a policy, and we know what to do, we should take such a request to the minister or other appropriate leader, so that a response can be agreed. It is far better to say to someone that we are unsure, and that we will make further enquiries, than either to agree or to refuse on the spot. Those with an experience of the Roman Catholic Church may associate anointing with preparation for dying. However, this understanding is narrower than intended, and in the Roman Catholic Church anointing is now referred to as the sacrament of life.

If a church wishes to explore the ministry of healing, on either an individual or a collective basis, many resources are available, with orders of service in a variety of denominational service books. However, the material provided by the Iona Community in their Worship Book as used by them in Iona Abbey explores healing and the laying on of hands in a very simple yet profound way, and in ways which will be accessible across a wide range of theological and ecclesiastical understandings. In the same way, their order of service and worship resources provide an approach which is helpful to many.

All through this book I have emphasized that those offering pastoral care do so as part of a team. No one has to tackle things by themselves, even though we may sometimes find ourselves in the position of having to give a first response. Should that situation arise, whether or not we have a prepared response ready for it, we should always feel able to say that we need to consult with the minister or other church leader as a matter of urgency.

Anyone who asks for laying on of hands or anointing is asking for ministry. We may not feel very comfortable with what is being asked for, but even a negative response must be offered in the spirit of ministry. We may feel that, for what seem to us to be very good reasons, after consultation, we cannot agree. If so, that refusal needs to be presented with very great care and sensitivity, or we may feel that this is not the time to refuse, whatever our own views, and therefore agree to laying on of hands or anointing but with some diffidence. We should always offer either response graciously and with kindness, because both responses are acts of faith not just for us but for the church. If we do proceed, we can be confident that God will neither reject our stumbling act of faith nor refuse to bless anyone seeking such a ministry. If we feel we have to say 'no', we must be confident that God will also honour that decision, and help us to continue to offer pastoral care to that person.

Some questions for personal reflection, or discussion with others

- Do you feel comfortable or uncomfortable around people who are ill?

- How do you feel about the suggestions that healing is more about wholeness than about curing?

- Is there anything in your own experience, positive or negative, which affects how you feel about offering pastoral care to people who are ill?

A prayer to use

Spirit of the living God, we know that you are present with us now. May your love enter us, and everyone for whom we pray, in body, mind and spirit. May we and all your people be healed of all that harms us. We ask this in the name and spirit of Jesus. Amen.

10

Caring in difficult situations

All Christians, and all churches, experience ups and downs in their faith and their relationships. This is not a new phenomenon – you only need to read the letters to the church in Corinth to see what a mess they ended up in. If we are offering pastoral care it is inevitable that at one time or another we will sometimes find ourselves trying to offer care in situations that are more complex or more traumatic than usual.

Once we have begun to offer pastoral care our encounters with people will soon teach us that people respond to us in different ways. To some people we will be a most welcome face and we will have a sense of developing friendship, but from others there may be no welcome forthcoming. In those situations, we may feel a sense of distance and may even begin to wonder if our pastoral work is doing more harm than good. Any rejection can arouse a variety of feelings in us. We may feel anxious about contacting anyone for the first time. We may feel hurt and find that memories of other more painful incidents in our lives have been stirred up. We may be feeling guilty that in some sense we are letting God, the church, other people or ourselves down. For most people it takes at least some of the shine off our ministry and may make us wonder if we were right to let ourselves offer pastoral care. We may even find ourselves asking if, or for how long, we can continue offering pastoral care.

No church leader ever is the perfect pastor for everyone in the congregation. Even the minister who seems very popular will have people in their churches who don't care for them, even if they never say so. In the same way, even an unpopular minister will have someone who appreciates them. No one person is God's answer for everyone. None of us can be 'all things to all people'. We should not be discouraged about this, because Jesus was certainly not liked by everyone! Jesus welcomed everyone, but not everyone welcomed him. We can hardly expect to manage greater popularity than Jesus did. This is what Jesus meant when he said to his disciples: 'Very truly, I tell you, servants are not greater than their master, nor are messengers greater than the one who sent them. If you know these things, you are blessed if you do them' (John 13.16–17).

In being asked to offer pastoral care, our gifts have been recognized by the church, and in a formal team the church has given us a level of authorization, and has promised to support and encourage us. The church has not said, and will never say to us, that we are going to be popular, or that we should measure the success of our pastoral care by popularity. However, all churches need to be sensitive when people offering pastoral care find things difficult or challenging, and how we support people in these situations needs to be part of our pastoral care system and structures, and our reviews of that.

It may not always feel this way, but the people to whom we try to offer pastoral care have been given to us by God. There are days when that will seem hard to believe, but this is the only way that we can ultimately make sense of ministry of pastoral care. The systems and structures that our church has for offering pastoral care were not chosen at random, but were thought through with care and prayer. This means that we need to be thankful for them. It is quite immaterial whether or not our personal relationship with them is good. Even if we feel the pain of rejection, we are still challenged to give thanks for people. In the most challenging situations, we can always remember what Jesus went through on the cross for us. Our calling and our challenge is to be thankful for the people in our care, thanking God for each person, irrespective of our own feelings about them.

Naturally, rejection is very painful. Jesus reminds us to 'Love your enemies and pray for those who persecute you' (Matthew

5.44) and Paul expands this when he says, 'Bless those who persecute you; bless and do not curse them' (Romans 12.14). If that was the teaching of Jesus, who faced persecution that led to his death, and of Paul who had done his share of the persecuting, we generally face considerably less challenging situations, and so to pray for blessing on those who reject us is what God asks us to try to do. It might just begin to make all the difference to them.

If our encounter with someone has left us feeling ill at ease, it is likely that it has also left them feeling uncomfortable. In their own way they may well reflect what we are feeling, and perhaps be confused. As part of our pastoral care for them we can ask God to use those feelings to create new possibilities.

Everyone offering pastoral care will certainly have times when they feel the strains of this ministry. To cope with this and to keep ourselves healthy, we will usually need to share our situation with others involved. Obviously, personal details of individual situations cannot be shared, but if we share the general situations that trouble us ('someone doesn't respond to me well', rather than 'Mabel is rude about me') with others offering pastoral care or with the ministers, we can seek the support that we need. In some situations this may be difficult, if there are clashes of personality or policy within the team, and we may be unsure where the cause for concern lies, or even if we ourselves are a part of the problem. In these situations, there might be value in consulting, in strict confidence, someone outside the situation.

Working as part of a team generally provides immense support when we see a need but cannot see the means to satisfy it. Clearly no individual has all the gifts and skills needed in some situations, and no church always has the full treasury of God within its own resources, yet we can find much more of this through partnership. We need to be willing to share what we have been given within appropriate confidentiality, and to feel able to ask others to share with us what troubles them. The benefit of being part of a team is that everyone can help each other.

CARING IN DIFFICULT SITUATIONS

One difficult situation is when people stop attending church, either suddenly or gradually. Our response will naturally be shaped by the personal relationship we have with them, but almost certainly there are other factors that we need to consider, such as why people have ceased to attend church. Have we asked, or have we assumed? Do we sense that our church should be able to provide for all the spiritual needs of the members, or do we sense that our church and its members have tides and seasons within which some people may sometimes move from one church to another to fulfil their potential? What roles do people play in the active life of the congregation?

Given the complex variety of situations, and individual reasons, it is not possible to offer any single approach that will cover all eventualities, but we can still have some kind of overall framework to help us. This framework will surely differ from church to church, not least because of the wide variety of differences in understanding both the nature of the local church and of Christian discipleship not just between different denominations, but within them. However, there are some elements which should be included in any approach we take.

We need to avoid assuming things. The dangers of assuming things are obvious. It is all too easy to assume that we know why people do the things they do. We need to hear as clearly as possible from the people themselves their real reasons for not coming to church. Only then, when we know what is really going on in their hearts and minds, can we be in any position to respond, and then only with care.

We do need to take people leaving the church seriously. It is a sad truth that all too often people drift away unnoticed. Churches try hard to support people in marriage crisis, people with disabilities, people in financial difficulties, people who have been bereaved, and we put a lot of time, effort and finance into helping them as individuals. Most churches sadly expend somewhat less effort on trying to help those passing through times of spiritual crisis, and those who drift away from church. All too often people who stop attending church are regarded as a problem for which the best approach is 'Least said, soonest mended', and where there have been unresolved tensions in the past this attitude is sometimes keen. In general, people drifting away from churches is a bad thing, which most churches would benefit from addressing more. It is of limited value recruiting new members through the front door, if the existing ones are creeping out of the back door. However, I am very clear that there are sometimes (limited) occasions when it is in everyone's best interests that someone leaves a church. Occasionally, all kinds of liberation can follow a departure. However, this is far from the norm, and any consideration of being better off without someone is always a last resort.

Many people will not feel comfortable sharing the depth of their feelings with us during a cursory conversation. If people are prepared to talk with us, we need to allow time, if they'll give it to us, to establish that we are for them. We should, therefore, expect that we might need more than conversation with them. All too often many of us have heard people reflecting on their links with the church in the past, and they disclose that no one ever bothered to ask why, if they even noticed. Their inference is that the fellowship to which they had given their allegiance and a portion of their lives did not care for them.

Whatever the truth of the matter, and there are always two sides to every story, while people say things with sincerity they do not always represent what actually happened at the time. Sadly, whatever actually happened or didn't happen, people feel that their expectations were not met or that the church failed them in some way. Therefore, the better our relationships with people that we care for, the sooner we speak to people when we miss them, the earlier we express our concern for them the better, especially if we go out of our way to do so. Leaving it until we happen to meet them in the supermarket will not convey the same message, even if the same words are used.

The process of leaving a church inevitably contains many pressures for everyone involved. Clearly there are pressures on those in leadership of the church, but we need to consider the pressures that other people might also be feeling. If our own relationship with them has been amicable, we will surely want to talk with them ourselves, but we need to recognize that most people are very reluctant to hurt others. If there is anything about us personally that has become a factor in their leaving the church, they may be acutely embarrassed if we ask them. For them, this may then make their feelings worse, potentially leading to evasion or feeling guilty, or more guilty than they may feel already. Similar forces can come into play where the church really feels that such matters are best left to the minister to deal with. People sometimes leave a church because they have problems with the way in which the church is being led, and if that is so then the very leader(s) with whom they are already dissatisfied is unlikely to be able to improve matters and may make it more difficult for the minister to minister effectively to them. In this situation, someone a little detached from events might be the person to offer a listening ear without a need to defend the leadership's position. If issues can be resolved, the way may be opened for people either to join actively once again in the life of the fellowship or to be released without guilt.

Even when people have good reasons for leaving a church, or for dropping responsibilities, they can still end up feeling guilty. Indeed, they may be angry because the church has made them feel guilty. If we express our, perfectly natural, concerns about how to find someone to replace them, we often mean this as an expression of serious appreciation for what someone has done, but sadly it is equally likely to be heard as an implication that they are letting the church down, and might well induce significant guilt. When people need to be released, however difficult we find it, we must make every effort to set them free as graciously as we are able to. This is naturally even more difficult to achieve in a small congregation but really our ability to induce guilt is probably just as great in any size of church. Making people feel guilty is not what we are supposed to be about, and best avoided.

Only when we know why people are no longer attending church might we be able to work out if or how we might be able to offer them pastoral care. Where people have made the decision to leave our church they will sometimes know where they are going. If they have made a link already with another church, they may neither need nor want any further involvement from us, but it is always courteous to ask them, even if they are leaving following a dispute. If they haven't made a link with another church, the offer of helping them to find one can be one way of enabling them to go in peace. This might, in fact, make a significant difference to how easy they find it to settle in another church, as unresolved conflicts are a poor foundation for new relationships. It is also worth observing that occasionally a person will join several churches in a town in succession, and eventually leave each one finding it wanting. If this happens to us, and we are some way down their list of churches, we should not take it too personally if we are eventually added to the list of churches tried and found wanting.

Sometimes people will simply stop attending services but with no intention at that time of leaving the church in the sense of resigning their membership. In this situation it is generally better to try to discover their reasons and then formulate our response specifically once we know these. If we engage with people in this kind of open way, then we have our best hope for a constructive relationship, and a constructive relationship is the best way to keep the door open for them to return to church life once again in the future.

Whose responsibility is it to maintain contact with people not attending the church services? This can often be a source of irritation in churches because it is often assumed that if people wish to keep some kind of link with the church, then the onus is upon them to do that. This often arises when a church is considering costs based on numbers, for people not attending may incur a cost for the church, to which they might not be contributing. Is it really just the responsibility of the non-attending to keep in touch? If we have accepted that there are legitimate reasons for us to support their position, the responsibility for providing the pastoral care that is needed to maintain their link with the church is then ours, not theirs. If we find ourselves writing people off, and never giving them the opportunity to come, then we have decided we don't want them to come. If they are not invited then they do not know of the opportunity to come, they do not know if they will be welcome if they do come; and they do not know that they have not been completely forgotten. It is important that we take the initiative. Clearly, frequently repeated invitations, especially to the same thing, can create unhelpful pressure or simply irritate, leaving people wondering if we really understand what they have said to us. However, never offering an invitation sends a very clear signal that no one cares about them. Sometimes, then, it might be helpful to everyone to agree with people a basis of continuing contact as one expression of our care for them, such as sending publications, and contact at major festivals. If we do make any such arrangement, then it is very important that we keep that up and do what we have said. The pastoral care that we seek to give people is supposed to be a reflection of the way that Jesus loves us. Jesus is a man of the utmost honour who does not break his promise. The way we deal with people tells them a lot about us, and if we do it well it should also tell them a lot about Jesus.

Everyone offering pastoral care, whether a new volunteer or a very experienced minister, will sometimes find moments when things go wrong, because we all make mistakes, sometimes grievous ones. Each of us knows without doubt that for every occasion on which this is true and known to others, there are more that are known to us alone. Sometimes we feel despondent, sad, unworthy, or inept for the ministry. Here are some initial thoughts to help us at these times:

1 We must accept that we are not perfect. We do not always do the right thing, even when we want to, because we are not God. Paul knew this when he wrote, 'For I do not do the good I want, but the evil I do not want is what I do' (Romans 7.19).

2 We must realize that God wants the best of us, and to help us do that, so we need to express to God our intention to try afresh, and to ask God to renew our resources.

3 In the normal course of offering pastoral care we shall know only too well when we have got it wrong, and it is always best to admit our responsibility freely.

4 We should avoid excuses, despite the temptation to offer them. Even when they are completely true, they give the unfortunate impression that we are trying to escape our responsibilities. In any event, people will spot what we are doing and begin to wonder what the actual truth of the matter is. They may even wonder what we are trying to cover up. We may well find that when it comes to taking responsibility for ourselves and for our actions we also begin to make excuses to God. Excuses, by implication, suggest we do not trust God to forgive us, but we can trust God: 'If we confess our sins, he who is faithful and just will forgive us our sins and cleanse us from all unrighteousness' (1 John 1.9).

When things go wrong, it's time to confess to God, apologize without excuses to people, and offer the whole situation to God, knowing that God is gracious, and then return to getting on with the job.

Some questions for personal reflection, or discussion with others

- Have you any experiences of people leaving a church?
- Does your church have a functional team offering pastoral care?
- Where do you look for support in difficult times?

A prayer to use

Living God, when relationships are strained or even broken, and we might feel inadequate, may your love and skill work through us to offer the hope of healing and wholeness. Where people may feel bruised or broken, help them to find release from their pain through freedom and peace. We ask this through Jesus Christ our Lord. Amen.

11

A reflection

After ten chapters of more practical thinking, the final part is a reflection which is offered to try to shape our work in a more spiritual context, lest we forget how much we rely upon God, and how God uses us even though we are imperfect. The reflection is based upon a passage from the prophet Isaiah.

> See, my servant shall prosper;
>   he shall be exalted and lifted up,
>   and shall be very high.
> Just as there were many who were astonished at him
>   – so marred was his appearance, beyond human semblance,
>   and his form beyond that of mortals –
> so he shall startle many nations;
>   kings shall shut their mouths because of him;
> for that which had not been told them they shall see,
>   and that which they had not heard they shall contemplate.
>
> Who has believed what we have heard?
>   And to whom has the arm of the Lord been revealed?
> For he grew up before him like a young plant,
>   and like a root out of dry ground;
> he had no form or majesty that we should look at him,
>   nothing in his appearance that we should desire him.
> He was despised and rejected by others;
>   a man of suffering and acquainted with infirmity;
> and as one from whom others hide their faces
>   he was despised, and we held him of no account.

A REFLECTION

Surely he has borne our infirmities
   and carried our diseases;
yet we accounted him stricken,
   truck down by God, and afflicted.
But he was wounded for our transgressions,
   crushed for our iniquities;
upon him was the punishment that made us whole,
   and by his bruises we are healed.
All we like sheep have gone astray;
   we have all turned to our own way,
and the Lord has laid on him
   the iniquity of us all.

He was oppressed, and he was afflicted,
   yet he did not open his mouth;
like a lamb that is led to the slaughter,
   and like a sheep that before its shearers is silent,
   so he did not open his mouth.
By a perversion of justice he was taken away.
   Who could have imagined his future?
For he was cut off from the land of the living,
   stricken for the transgression of my people.
They made his grave with the wicked
   and his tomb with the rich,
although he had done no violence,
   and there was no deceit in his mouth.

Yet it was the will of the Lord to crush him with pain.
When you make his life an offering for sin,
   he shall see his offspring, and shall prolong his days;
through him the will of the Lord shall prosper.
   Out of his anguish he shall see light;
he shall find satisfaction through his knowledge.
   The righteous one, my servant, shall make many righteous,
   and he shall bear their iniquities.
Therefore I will allot him a portion with the great,
   and he shall divide the spoil with the strong;

because he poured out himself to death,
  and was numbered with the transgressors;
yet he bore the sin of many,
  and made intercession for the transgressors.

Isaiah 52.13–53.12

The brutal truth of life is that at one time or another we have all been wounded by pain. Some of us have scars on our bodies, some have scars on our minds, and some scars on soul or our spirit. We do not have to look too deep within ourselves or others to understand that we are all wounded at one level or another.

I wonder how God wants us to handle our wounds? Is there hope for those who are wounded? I believe very firmly that there is hope, that healing and wholeness are possible. And this hope begins with our willingness to heal the wounds of others. What I mean is that in our own woundedness we can be a source of life for others, or, to put it another way, we can become wounded healers.

What on earth does a wounded healer mean? The answer begins in Jesus, where our faith begins. In Jesus, we see the personification of total love that suffered and was wounded on the cross. Isaiah describes how much the servant suffered, and those ugly and painful wounds remind us of just how wounded we are.

Many of us might think that being wounded ourselves makes it difficult for us to help other people, but actually that's the point. Being able to understand is what enables us to help. This is what being a wounded healer is all about – being able to connect and identify with other people who are also wounded and say, 'I understand. I have been wounded too. How can I help?'

Over the years, I have learned that an awful lot of people want to be listened to more than anything else, as they work out their own problems and solutions. Not always, of course, but it is about a listening ear as much as anything else. Listening with an understanding ear, an attentive ear, a safe ear, a caring ear, is what many people are seeking. We do have two ears, but only one mouth, and helping people is very often as much as about listening and being as it is about doing. As Paul put it: 'Bear one another's burdens, and in this way you will fulfil the law of Christ' (Galatians 6.2).

If we can find our way to help others despite, or because of, our own wounds, we can actually help to heal our own wounds. People with addictions often find themselves leading twelve-step groups to help other people. A retired minister who had been very ill with cancer set up a local support group and through helping others found themselves helped. These kinds of things to help others are so often the means by which our own wounds have been healed.

In his novel *A Farewell to Arms*, Ernest Hemingway writes of how everyone is broken by the world, but after that they become strong at the places where they were broken. If you glue pieces of wood together many wood glues claim that the glue is stronger than the wood itself, and what they mean is that the repair is stronger than the original. This is what happens to people, and that is what Hemingway meant. We become strong at the broken places. And that is what being wounded healers means. We become strong at the broken places of our lives. Our wounds begin to heal because they are being used to give comfort and strength to others.

Some years ago, there was a very popular song sung by Bette Midler titled, 'From A Distance'. The chorus said, 'God is watching us from a distance.' The song had a great message, which spoke of God seeing our troubled world, but the suggestion that God is watching us from a distance is nonsense. In Jesus, God came right here in the midst of us, carrying the burdens of the world. In Jesus, God suffers with us in the midst of our woundedness. We do not worship or follow a God who does not know and understand what it is like to be wounded. Isaiah was writing of a God who is wounded for us and who is wounded with us, making God the ultimate wounded healer. In Jesus, God became one of us and became wounded like the rest of us. And it is through Jesus that we understand that God is intimately connected to us and is deeply impacted by the care and compassion that we attempt to give even to the least among us.

If anyone was the incarnation of this truth, it was Mother Teresa. When she heard that there were people in Calcutta dying in the streets because the religious culture said they were 'untouchable', she dedicated her whole life to helping them. She went to Calcutta, built a hospital, and went out to the streets to find those who were dying of disease and malnutrition. She would bring them to the hospital where they could be held, rocked, prayed for, and loved. Then she told them about the love of Christ. Some got better, and some died in her arms. Her description of her work was simply, 'What you do for them, you also do for him.'

If we look around, in church, in our families, in our community, we see the wounded, the sick, the lonely, the hungry, the thirsty, and the depressed. If we are able to reach out with our wounds to heal their wounds, we may just see the face of Christ and realize that we are healing the wounds of Christ. What you do for them, you also do for him.

Some questions for personal reflection, or discussion with others

- Are you aware of wounds in yourself and others?
- To what extent do you see Jesus as a wounded healer?
- In what sense can you accept that helping others can also help you?

A prayer to use

Jesus, as a wounded healer you reveal your own sufferings to us, and we know your scars. Through them, bring comfort to everyone who is suffering body, mind or spirit, that any anguish, strife and despair may be transformed into health and wholeness. In your name we pray. Amen.

Suggestions for further reading

If you have found this book helpful or thought-provoking, and want to explore more, you could try:

Kate Lichfield, *Tend My Flock: Sustaining Good Practice in Pastoral Care*, Canterbury Press, 2006.
Michael Forster, *Being There: The Healing Power of Presence*, Kevin Mayhew, 2015.

If you are looking for more detailed guidance or support with particular topics, SPCK publish a long-running series 'Library of Pastoral Care', with books on every possible subject.

Index of Bible References

Old Testament

Psalms

Psalm 92.1	41
Psalm 121.4	7

Isaiah

Isaiah 52.13–53.12	88–90

New Testament

Matthew

Matthew 5.44	79
Matthew 10.12	43
Matthew 10.19–20	43
Matthew 25.35–36	48

Luke

Luke 4.18–19	26
Luke 9	48

John

John 13.16–17	79
John 13.34	10
John 13.35	11

Romans

Romans 7.19	85
Romans 8.26–28	40
Romans 12.14	80

1 Corinthians

1 Corinthians 1.25	5

2 Corinthians

2 Corinthians	48

Galatians

Galatians 4.19	3
Galatians 6.2	91
Galatians 6.10	37

Ephesians

Ephesians 3.18–19	33
Ephesians 4.15	3

Philippians

Philippians 1.6	3

Colossians		*1 Peter*	
Colossians 1.28	12	1 Peter 2.9–10	2
Hebrews		*1 John*	
Hebrews 4.14–15	40	1 John 1.9	86
		1 John 4.19	12
James			
James 5	73–6		

Index of Names and Subjects

Age 4, 21, 24, 54–63
Anointing 72, 73–6

Bias 23–4

Calling 1–3
Charter for children in the church 63–4
Children 12, 15–17, 24, 25, 26, 54–63
Commitment 12, 13, 16, 58, 74
Communication 12
Confidentiality 13, 38, 50, 80

Difficult situations 78–87
Disability 16, 21, 27–8

Early Church 12
Equality 20, 21, 26, 29, 30, 63

Families 54–63
Friendship 5, 32–3, 34, 36, 37, 47, 48, 60, 78

Gender 16, 21, 28–9, 61

Hands, laying on 72, 73–6
Hemingway, Ernest 91

Holy Communion 69, 72

Language 22–3, 28–9, 51
LGBTQIA+ people 30–1

Marriage 21, 81
Midler, Bette 91
Mistakes 16, 85–6

Offering 6–7

Pastoral care, definition 10–14
Pastoral care, effectiveness 1, 3, 4, 13, 22, 24, 26, 44, 56, 62, 71, 72
Pastoral care, patterns 10, 46, 47
People, understanding 20–35
Poverty 24–6
Prayer 9, 11, 14, 20, 36–45, 59, 62, 69, 70, 71, 72, 74, 79

Race 16, 21, 29–30
Receiving 8–9
Reflection 88–92
Refugees 31
Religion or belief 16, 21

Safeguarding ix, 1, 15–19, 22, 30, 46, 55, 61, 90
Self-care 4–9
Sex 21, 28–9
Sick people 65–77
Skills 6–7
Support 4–9, 13, 15, 17, 18, 21, 22, 29, 40, 51, 56, 59, 60, 62, 68, 71, 72, 73, 79, 86

Teresa, Mother 92
Time 4–5

Visiting 7, 11, 37, 41, 46–53, 64, 65, 66, 68, 69

Wounded healers 88–92

www.ingramcontent.com/pod-product-compliance
Lightning Source LLC
Chambersburg PA
CBHW031126080526
44587CB00011B/1129